GROWING UP
TRANS

In Our Own Words

Edited by

Dr. Lindsay Herriot and Kate Fry

ORCA BOOK PUBLISHERS

Published in Canada and the United States in 2021 by Orca Book Publishers.
orcabook.com

Library and Archives Canada Cataloguing in Publication
Title: Growing up trans : in our own words /
edited by Dr. Lindsay Herriot and Kate Fry.
Names: Herriot, Lindsay, editor. | Fry, Kate, editor.
Description: Includes bibliographical references.
Identifiers: Canadiana (print) 20210105569 |
Canadiana (ebook) 20210105607 | ISBN 9781459831377 (softcover) |
ISBN 9781459831384 (PDF) | ISBN 9781459831391 (EPUB)
Subjects: LCSH: Transgender youth. | LCSH: Transgender people. |
LCSH: Transgender people's writings.
Classification: LCC HQ77.9 .G76 2021 | DDC j305.23086/7—dc23

Library of Congress Control Number: 2020924190

Summary: This illustrated nonfiction anthology is a collection of
stories, essays, poetry and art by transgender youth.

Orca Book Publishers is committed to reducing the consumption of nonrenewable resources in
the making of our books. We make every effort to use materials that support a sustainable future.

Orca Book Publishers gratefully acknowledges the support for its publishing programs provided
by the following agencies: the Government of Canada, the Canada Council for the Arts and the
Province of British Columbia through the BC Arts Council and the Book Publishing Tax Credit.

Cover image: Self-Portrait by Ajam
Editor photos: Jae Levy
Cover and interior design: Dahlia Yuen
In-house editor: Kirstie Hudson

Printed and bound in Canada.

24 23 22 21 • 1 2 3 4

To trans youth—
past, present and future

Contents

Bodies

Everyday Life

Schools

Mental Health

Acceptance

Afterword

DYLAN ARIAWAN, age 18,
+ ELLIOTT KHAN, age 10

An early name of the Gender Generations Project was the Trans Tipping Point. This Trans Tipping Point logo was created in a day and started with the yin-and-yang design of two elements. We specifically chose the transgender and nonbinary flags to represent the organization because most of the participants identify in the transgender and nonbinary spectrum. The community focuses more on the experience of gender than sexuality, so it is a safe space for all to relate to one another.

Introduction

Welcome.

This book began as a conversation, and we hope that it will spark many more. Waiting for the Vancouver SkyTrain one otherwise ordinary morning, we (Lindsay and Kate) talked about how it seemed that stories about young, **transgender** lives framed them in only two ways, as tragedy or triumph. We knew from our trans family and friends that there are so many ways to be young and trans and wished there were a book that represented the experiences of many different trans youth. *Growing Up Trans: In Our Own Words* was born out of that conversation and out of a need for lots more conversations and representations of what young trans life is like. Recognizing how **cisgender** adults tend to do most of the talking about trans youth, we wondered how we might help trans youth speak for themselves instead. The goal was not to "give" trans youth a voice—they already have one— but rather to use our cis, adult **privilege** to make those voices louder.

We coordinated three weekend-long writing retreats for trans youth from across Canada at the University of Victoria and the Fairfield Gonzales Community Association, on the unceded traditional territories of the Lekwungen peoples, in Victoria, British Columbia. A team of all-trans adult mentors—ranging from emerging to established artists, authors, activists and scholars—applied to come and teach, while we and a team of volunteers tended to tender hearts and washed the dishes. The result of those retreats is this book, which is a humble addition to the growing body of work by and for trans youth.

This collection presents a spectrum of life experiences from trans youth under the age of 18. Their stories are told in art, poetry, fiction, memoir, letters and essays. Some of the stories might feel heavy, while others are lighthearted or even a bit silly. Some of them might introduce you to ideas you've never thought about before, while others might feel all too familiar. Some might even do all of the above! Throughout the chapters, we (Lindsay and Kate) ask questions that will help you reflect on the stories and draw connections to your own life, regardless of your **gender identity**. Each section concludes with a response by an adult scholar in transgender studies, offering tips and advice for what readers can do next. There's also a list of books we love, organized by genre, so that readers of all ages and abilities can "choose their own adventure" in learning more about the themes from each chapter.

Not every reader will see their own experiences reflected back to them. Although there's a variety of young authors and artists in this book, they reflect a small part of the trans youth experience. In addition, most of the authors and artists are from Coast Salish territories in British Columbia, as that is where the program was located. Thankfully, this is not the final word on young trans life, either in Canada or elsewhere. *Growing Up Trans: In Our Own Words* is instead a modest first step in starting more conversations and telling more stories. It's a sample of some, but certainly not all, or even most, of the stories about what it might be like to grow up trans. We're optimistic that this is the beginning of many more published works by trans youth, and we invite readers to start dreaming up, drafting and diversifying version 2.0.

Enjoy.

—DR. LINDSAY HERRIOT + KATE FRY

Growing Up Trans began as a one-year writing project that grew into the Trans Tipping Point and then became the Gender Generations Project, an ongoing íntentional, ***intersectional*** and intergenerational collective. It puts all trans, ***nonbinary, Two-Spirit*** and otherwise non-cisgender youth in the fullness of all their identities at the center of the project. We welcome mentors, volunteers and their loved ones to build gender joy. Entirely trans-led and headquartered on unceded territories of the Lekwungen peoples, in Victoria, British Columbia, we offer free services, programming, and volunteer and paid-work opportunities year-round. Please visit gendergenerations.org for more information. The royalties from the sale of this book will be donated to the Gender Generations Project to further their work.

and the mauve ones
are boys,

and the white ones
are girls,

and the blue ones
are just little
sillies who are not
sure what they are.

-Peter Pan
J.M.Barrie

The Blue Fairy

AJAM, age 14, + OWEN MILLER, age 16

Childhood

Do you have specific childhood memories of learning about or playing with gender? For example, do you remember any games or toys you were told you should or shouldn't play/play with because of your gender?

How do TV, movies and video games aimed at kids portray the differences between boys and girls (which is sometimes called the *gender binary*)? If you could make changes to the way gender is represented in the media, what would they be?

How can adults help shape the way kids think about gender?

That's how it feels sometimes.
Somebody spun my cubes
And I'm all mixed up.

—*Asa O'Connor-Jaeckel*

Mixed-Up

ASA O'CONNOR-JAECKEL, age 13

Have you seen
Those children's toys?
The ones at kids' sections
In libraries
Or in daycares.
The ones with three cubes
On a vertical pole
That you can spin around.

On each side of the cube
Is the head, body or feet
Of a cartoon animal.
If you spin the cubes in
Different directions
You can get a mixed-up body
Of an animal.
The lines will match up
But the rest won't fit.
That's how it feels sometimes.
Somebody spun my cubes
And I'm all mixed up.
But the rest of me isn't on
Those cubes.

Pink Herrings

CHRISTOPHER, age 17

The doctor's office feels perfectly square
A cubic terrarium for one anomaly
When he leans forward and says to me,
"Surely there must've been signs."

I say, "Surely there must've been, sir,
But when I was an infant, I didn't know how to speak."
Funny how infants can be—
And between all the gibberish and crying
(Though maybe I cried because I was so misaligned)
It was difficult to distinguish the babbling from the prophecy.

"Surely there must've been signs, sir,
When I clambered from the crib to the playground
And built a new identity out of sand and mismatched Legos.
Surely it was obvious: boy now, boy then.
But I was also a velociraptor
And a dragon tamer
And a space captain.

"Surely there must've been signs,
But when I wasn't out hunting outlaws
I was having tea parties with the plush cavalier
In an empire of rosy sheets and dollhouse furniture
Painting butterflies, humming lullabies
Not knowing that signs cancel out signs.

"Sir, I'm sure there were signs
Lost amongst these pink herrings
And I'll dig up each one if that's what it takes
But what better sign than me sitting here now?
And I can't help but wonder what difference it makes."

Trapped

DAVID LLEWELYN, age 14

Avatars

LUPUS, age 14

This piece is dedicated to all those who could not be freed from their cage, and to the people strong enough to break through.

Have you ever heard of the video games *The Sims 4* or *IMVU (I Am Virtual You)*? Well, they are both avatar games—games in which you create your own character. The best thing about these games is that your character can be anything...in the binary world of Male and Female. Do you ever see those *Game of War* advertisements with the blond lady that has big breasts? What about *GTA (Grand Theft Auto)* games, where all the young guys have six-packs or eight-packs and huge muscles? I'm not saying that it's wrong for every character (male or female) to have Barbie/Ken figures. It's just unrealistic.

Personally, I don't mind the gender binary in some of these games. I find fake virtual males with lots of muscles kind of attractive. At least they are somewhat achievable and realistic for real humans. (Everybody is different; don't feel bad if you don't have big bulky muscles.) On the other hand, in every single game I've seen with female avatars, all the avatars have big butts and breasts and teeny-tiny waists. I probably don't like that idea because I'm not attracted to females, although it could also be my view of a reflection of what society thinks women should look like. Whatever it is, I don't approve.

In contrast, in the game *The Sims 4* you can create your own virtual characters that can range from fat to skinny, buff to bony, etc. However, the game still stays within the gender binary. I don't think that many game developers actually know what the term *nonbinary* means, but the game still gives all types of clothing for both sexes/genders. I know clothes aren't the only thing that contributes to a nonbinary individual, but it's a pretty great option to have a variety of clothing to choose from. When designing a character, you can adjust their size, shape and every little detail of every little thing about them. That leaves you with your own personally designed character, fit to your taste. (God, I sound like I'm writing a game review.)

I really love these games because I get to create a "me" that I like. This character is the person I see in the mirror. This character is what I hope to someday be. To be truthful, I'm already halfway there. I have been most of my life, because on the inside, I already am that avatar.

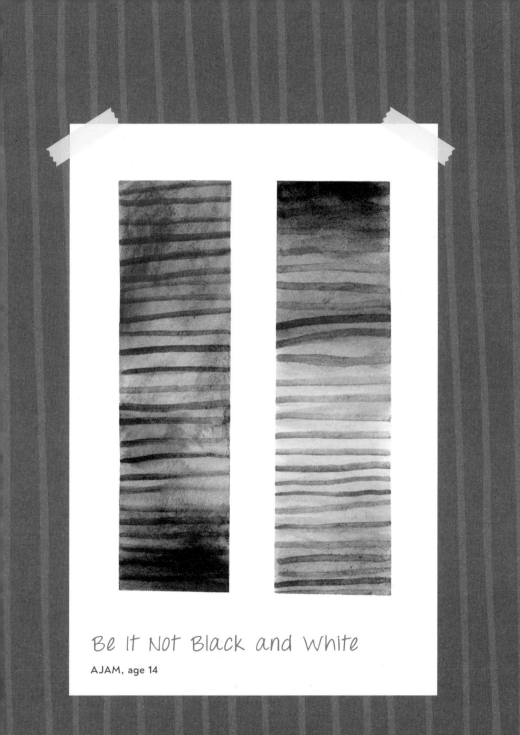

Be It Not Black and White

AJAM, age 14

It can be really hurtful to hear someone misgender or misname you, and it's often hard to stand up for yourself. Sometimes it's easier to do it for someone else.

—*Christopher Wolff*

What Can I Do Now?

CHRISTOPHER WOLFF, trans writer, facilitator and educator

1. **Ask non-gendered questions about babies.** When someone you know is having a baby, you can ask all sorts of questions instead of "Is it a boy or a girl?" You could ask such questions as: "When is the baby due?" "Do you have a name picked out?" "Are you planning any special celebrations to welcome the new baby?" "How are you feeling?" You can also give cards, gifts and balloons that don't say *boy* or *girl* and aren't pink or blue.

2. **Stand up for your friends and have them stand up for you.** It can be really hurtful to hear someone **misgender** or misname you, and it's often hard to stand up for yourself. Sometimes it's easier to do it for someone else. Why not support your friend when they get misgendered? Say, "Excuse me, my friend's **pronouns** are…" or "My friend's name is…" And your friend can do the same for you when it happens to you. Together you are stronger!

3. **Think about who gets to make art.** Who are your favorite trans artists? What do they look like? Do they look like you and your friends? Sometimes there are certain expectations on trans people to look like cis people in order to be successful. Remember that all trans people are valid and important, no matter what their *transition* looks like. It's important to have variety in the community! Celebrate all art by all artists.

4. **Use your library.** The library in your community is a great place to learn more about other trans people's stories (see our list called What Do I Read Next at the end of each chapter to get you started). You might also ask how the library can become more friendly to trans people. Do they have all-genders washrooms? Do they accept chosen names on library cards? Are they putting on trans-centered events? These are just a few examples of how you could advocate for trans and nonbinary folks

5. **Practice pronouns.** Everyone makes mistakes when they're learning new pronouns and especially when they're learning how to use they/them for the first time. It can take time. Just like when someone changes their name after getting married or divorced, it takes time. When someone reminds you that you've used the wrong name or pronoun, they're not saying you're a bad person or that you don't care about trans people, and you definitely shouldn't beat yourself up about it. Just gracefully apologize, use the correct name or pronoun and move on.

What Can I Read Next?

PICTURE BOOKS

Gonzalez, Maya Christina, and Matthew Sg. *They, She, He, Easy as ABC*. San Francisco, CA: Reflection Press, 2019.

Ismail, Yasmeen. *I'm a Girl!* London, UK: Bloomsbury, 2016.
*Also available in French

Kaylani, Juanita, and Kyle Lukoff. *When Aiden Became a Brother*. New York, NY: Lee & Low Books, 2019.

YA AND GRAPHIC NOVELS

Boteju, Tanya. *Kings, Queens, and In-Betweens*. New York, NY: Simon Pulse, 2019.

Labelle, Sophie. *Ciel*. Toronto, ON: Second Story Press, 2020.
*Also available in French

GENERAL AUDIENCE

Meadow, Tey. *Trans Kids: Being Gendered in the Twenty-First Century*. Oakland, CA: University of California Press, 2018.

Ryle, Robyn. *She/He/They/Me: For the Sisters, Misters, and Binary Resisters*. Naperville, IL: Sourcebooks Inc., 2019.

MEMOIRS/FIRST-PERSON NARRATIVES

Kobabe, Maia. *Gender Queer: A Memoir*. Portland, OR: Oni Press, 2019.

Lohman, Eric, and Stephani Lohman. *Raising Rosie: Our Story of Parenting an Intersex Child*. London, UK: Jessica Kingsley Publishers, 2018.

Family

AJAM, age 14

Families

What expectations does your family have of you or other family members based on gender? Are there certain responsibilities women in your family have that men do not, or vice versa?

In what ways do the pieces in this chapter highlight the importance of family for transgender youth?

Can you think of other areas in which family acceptance is important for you? For example, is it important in such life choices as choosing friends or hobbies?

I muster the courage
to tell them
They had a boy
not a girl
They ignore it
What happened to
not caring
As long as I'm healthy?

—*Max*

As Long as I'm Healthy

MAX, age 13

Do you want a boy or a girl?
I don't care
as long as it's healthy
Then I was born
A little girl
They were happy
But later in life
I realize
I'm not a girl
but a boy
I stop eating regularly
I don't get enough sleep
I hate myself
Why can't I be normal?
Eventually,
I muster the courage to tell them
They had a boy
not a girl
They ignore it
What happened to
not caring
As long as I'm healthy?

Daddy's Little Girl

DANNY CHARLES, age 17

The doctor painted me pink when I wanted to be blue.

My dad wanted me to be the princess for Halloween.
He would dress me in pink fluffy dresses when I wanted to
be a cool boy ninja.
He would give me the sparkly pink wand when I wanted the
cool nunchucks or a big sword.

When I told him I wanted to transition to be a boy, the dread
on his face seemed like he lost his little girl, like his little girl
just vanished right in front of him, like his little girl just died
in his arms.

I kept saying, "I'm sorry," realizing now I shouldn't have
been sorry.

I remember I used to be your whole world, but then you left
without saying goodbye.

I never wanted to be a princess,
I never liked the big fluffy dresses,
I never liked the wand,
I never liked being ladylike.

I'm showing everyone I can be a better man than he will ever be.

Never be sorry for who you are; everyone in the LGBTQ2S+ community will be standing behind you and will hold you up when you can't hold yourself up.

The doctor painted me pink when I wanted to be blue.

—Danny Charles

Never be sorry for who you are; everyone in the LGBTQ2S+ community will be standing behind you and will hold you up when you can't hold yourself up.

—*Danny Charles*

Be Strong like Windows

SAMUEL BUSCH, age 17

I got glass stuck in my shoes
I got glass stuck in my teeth
Trying to speak is like cracking down on crime, my every
rebellious thought an offense to a **patriarch** more ingrained
in western culture than the shards in my gums
And even in your own home you'd expect, without tracking
the glass inside, you could walk bare or sock footed with no
need to tread lightly, but no.
The eggshells, landmines or whatever analogy you like stalks
you to sanctuary.

However feminist you proclaim or may be, my kind is still
included in those you are meant to advocate for
I am all boy
Not yet man
If you look for man, blink once, blink twice
You will miss him looking for the **misogynist** your father is.

(And I had to explain what misogyny was to you)

You don't hear about my victories
because you shook your head when people asked who this
young man with you was

when they said "he"
when they say "he"

you get frustrated that people see me as male with a costume
change and a haircut
'cause that's how fragile these social constructions are

you didn't hear about when I got through going to the bathroom for the first time
or when I called the doctor after two years walking barefoot
on broken glass with both of us digging our heels in
crushed pieces, making sand with the relational friction and
societal tension.

I'd always laugh to myself when I saw trans guys' bios that
said "self-made man"
but it makes sense now.
I did this myself, every stitch, every goddamn rhinestone
I trained my voice down
I did the research
I made the composition of language that aligns with my
inner feelings
I did the work
I did some work, though work was not needed and I was
enough,
the world required me to look male enough
and I achieve that most days

but this is my body and this is my life
the only one to carry me through sweet and strife
The only one I get to be held in by my boy, partner or wife

I'd like to be happy in it.
just as you hope for yourself.
It's not easy being this transparent about my emotions
but it's necessary for me to survive.
To be all cellophane and windowpanes
all clear wrap and cleaned glass

I will be made crystal under pressure.
I am precious.

You Always Wanted A Girl

ASA O'CONNOR-JAECKEL, age 13

Do her hair and
Understand her
Rarely have to
Reprimand her
Thoughtful child
Caring child
Sparkly, pink
Dress-wearing child

You always wanted a girl

And then your
Very first glimpse
Of me
The labia on
The ultrasound
Screen
The sign that,
For you, clearly
Spoke
The news for which
You'd dared not
Hope

You always wanted a girl

After the birth
Amid the stress
The surgeries
The five-month
Mess
The one thing you
Could no doubt
Say
The one thing that
Had gone
Your way
Was that you had
Got your wish

You always wanted a girl

I know that you
Would want no
Other
I know you
Mean it when
You say
That you are the
Luckiest
Mother
I know all this
With my whole heart
I know
As well
There was once
That part

That always wanted a girl

Prejudice Candle

YAKUSINN DEBOER, age 18

The world probably won't stay dumb forever, but **transphobia** is ticking down quite slowly. So why watch it burn away slowly when you can torch it straight from the bottom with your own hands? That's exactly what this scratch board and digital piece is, except these hands are represented by a large fire-breathing dragon.

What Can I Do Now?

KYLE SHAUGHNESSY, social worker and writer

1. **Make sure to care for yourself too.** It's okay to love your trans friend or family member and still feel unsure about the right thing to do. Gender is joyful, but it can also be confusing. When families and friends feel supported, they can better support a beloved trans youth. So find communities, either online or in person, of other supportive allies where you can make mistakes, ask awkward questions, grieve, rage, grow and improve. Your school's Gender and Sexuality Alliance (GSA) or Parents and Friends of Lesbians and Gays (PFLAG) are great places to start. See the resources section of this book for a list of resources to help you find a community that's right for you or start your own.

2. **Know when to keep it simple.** You don't have to be a world expert in gender to support your trans friend—chances are they aren't an expert either! Start with empathy and nonjudgmental curiosity and let them take the lead. When you mess up, don't make it a big thing—just apologize and move on. Compassion and a willingness to try are much more important than knowing all the finer points of gender jargon.

3. **Recognize that family rejection comes in many forms.** Just because a young trans person has a roof over their head does not mean that they are safe, and it does not mean that this roof is permanent or unconditional. Look closely and consider overall wellness and safety in the wider sense. It may not be safe or wise to urge youth to leave the family home, so having a clearer picture of what they're going through guides us in our work to help buffer them from the harms.

4. **Honor chosen and original families.** Families are where we find belonging and kinship, are challenged to be and become our best selves, and are safe to come home to from the world (literally and figuratively). Families are where someone "gets" us at least some of the time. Families also grow and change over time, adding new members and losing others. Sometimes the ones we consider family aren't from our family of origin but are loved ones, friends, community members and others with whom we cross paths and relate to along the way—a chosen family, or family of meaning. Our family of meaning doesn't have to replace our family of origin, but for some of us it will, and it's just as valid and valued as a family of origin. Families look however we need them to.

5. **Know when and who to call for help.** No one expects you to know everything about how to support your young trans friend or family member. It's okay to ask for outside support from educators, healthcare providers and other affirming people and groups like counselors, social workers, youth groups, religious organizations and so on. Some are listed in the resources section of this book. Listen to your heart, trust your gut and ask for help when you need it.

You don't have to be a world expert in gender to support your trans friend—chances are they aren't an expert either!

—*Kyle Shaughnessy*

What Can I Read Next?

PICTURE BOOKS

Adeyoha, Angel. *The Zero Dads Club*. Toronto, ON: Flamingo Rampant, 2015.

Shraya, Vivek. *The Boy & the Bindi*. Vancouver, BC: Arsenal Pulp Press, 2016.

YA AND GRAPHIC NOVELS

Belge, Kathy, and Marke Bieschke. *Queer: The Ultimate LGBTQ Guide for Teens*. Minneapolis, MN: Zest Books, 2019.

McAdam, Tash. *Blood Sport*. Victoria, BC: Orca Book Publishers, 2020.

GENERAL AUDIENCE

Miller, LeeAndra, and Lindsay Elin. *Families in Transition: A Resource Guide for Families of Transgender Youth*, 2nd ed. Toronto, ON: Central Toronto Youth Services Publications, 2020.

*Also available in French

Nealy, Elijah C. *Transgender Children and Youth: Cultivating Pride and Joy with Families in Transition*. New York: W.W. Norton & Company, 2017.

MEMOIRS/FIRST-PERSON NARRATIVES

Jetté Knox, Amanda. *Love Lives Here: A Story of Thriving in a Transgender Family*. Toronto, ON: Penguin Random House Canada, 2019.

Thom, Kai Cheng. *Fierce Femmes and Notorious Liars: A Dangerous Trans Girl's Confabulous Memoir*. Montreal, QC: Metonymy Press, 2016.

Reflection

AJAM, age 14

Bodies

When do you feel most at home in your (gendered) body? What do you do that makes you feel at home in your body?

How might a person's gender identity or expression affect their mental health?

How is the language we use to talk about bodies gendered? Do words like "tough" or "cute" mean different things when applied to different genders?

Hair Expression

TOR BROUGHTON, age 12

Flip back six years, I cut off around twelve inches of hair, leaving me with a bob. That was an insane moment for me. My hair has become a big part of my identity as a person and a significant part of my **gender expression**.

In the summer of 2016, I dyed my hair red and cut it into the haircut that my friends and I have now nicknamed the volcano. Yes, the top was red and in a faux-hawk and the sides were brown and buzzed. I did indeed look like a volcano. I also got references to murder scenes about the red. At the time, I got a lot of compliments on it and thought I looked incredible. As I look back on it, it might not have been the best choice…

Luckily, that isn't where my hair journey ended. I let the top grow out, cut out the red and left my hair in a loose comb-over. Once again dyed the top, this time, blond. Buzzed the sides again and left them brown.

There were lots of side buzzes. Buzz, grow, buzz, grow, the same pattern. I can't handle having my sides longer than a pinkie nail. It drives me insane. So I get them buzzed down the shortest they can be without being bald. I then repeat that habit every three weeks. Buzz, grow, buzz, grow.

I went between a lot of stages of my hair throughout the years. From super-long hair down to my waist to a bob cut to some weird, emo-looking fringe haircut to a faux-hawk to where I am today, a loose comb-over.

My hair represents a large part of me and my identity. For most of my life, I've used my hair as a form of expressing my gender, as well as my personality. As I began realizing my gender identity, I also began exploring different hairstyles, and the two have now almost interlocked for me.

Because my hair is so closely bonded with me, I take pride in it. Even when I've made definite mistakes, such as the volcano. So when I'm teased or messed with because of my hair, it tends to hit deeper than it might for others. My hair is me, and that's who I am.

We are done concealing our true identities
We fly high and free, and feel
warm sun in our wings
But we butterflies are sensitive
An insult causes us to wilt and fall
So be kind to us, and cherish us
For we do not last forever

—*Maisie Bodrug*

Butterflies

MAISIE BODRUG, age 13

We used to be ugly caterpillars
Sad at not being who we truly are
Stress eating until we are self-conscious of our weight

When the time comes, we hide in our delicate chrysalis
Away from the abuse of the outside world
Preparing to bloom into a magnificent being and show our
true colors

We are done concealing our true identities
We fly high and free, and feel warm sun in our wings

But we butterflies are sensitive
An insult causes us to wilt and fall
So be kind to us, and cherish us
For we do not last forever

I wish I could wave a wand and make people suck a lot less, but that's just how we are. Some of us are super great in some ways, and some of us are super terrible in other ways.

—*A.J. Gabriel*

Dysphoria

A.J. GABRIEL, age 17

Is **[gender] *dysphoria*** kicking your ass right now? Yeah, me too. Here's some things I think about when I feel something isn't matching.

Little disclaimer: I have a tendency to cope with dysphoria through humor quite often. Something that has sprung from it is my ever-growing list of bizarre and just simply childish terms I use when referring to certain body parts. I hope that my awful innuendos are not too much to handle in this light read on coping with dysphoria.

I also cope with a hell of a lot of excessive self-love and self-congratulatory ideals. Sometimes it's hard to love yourself or to pretend you think you're deserving of self-love—but trust me, sometimes you're gonna be upset with yourself but that doesn't make you any less deserving of love.

Body Dysphoria

That body? It's on a cutie. That's you. Ur cute.

Love it. Are you missing parts or have ones you don't want? That's okay. Sometimes when you build furniture from a certain Nordic-themed store, they give you extra pieces that don't make sense, or they forget one or two. That's okay—it just is something that makes you, well, *you!*

Boobs? On a guy? That's wild. Look at those squishy pillows! Heck yeah!

A boob? Two boobs!? WOW! That's pretty freaking wild, my pal! Wait, are you missing boobs? Ah, heck, it be like that... but hey, you can save your back and shoulders, so if you got removable boobies, that's okay! If you got none, that's also okay! Not everyone has boobs, and that's completely fine!

Where's my dick?

Sometimes I get a weird feeling because I don't have the *ahem* *pee-pee* that I wish I'd been born with. It's weird to have or not have the parts you wish you had, and honestly, it can be an intense dysphoric feeling sometimes. If you are able to, I definitely recommend getting a packer or an STP (stand-to-pee) device if you are feeling the lack of a dong. Even just stuffing a pair of balled-up socks in your pants can give you a little bulge and that makes it feel less awkward. Be warned: I have had my packer fall out of my pant leg once, and that was horrifying, so be sure that everything is secured when you are wearing your devices! Avoid embarrassing situations at all costs... *like, oops, my no-no carrot took a tumble...out of my pants... oh well, that's just how it is sometimes, I guess.* If you unfortunately are stuck with having said appendage, gaffs are great! They even make ones with outlined labia on them, so that's pretty nifty too!

Curvy? A boy with curves? You bet your bottom dollar that's what I am!

Bodies come in all shapes and sizes! Do you think we're gonna just let you hate it? Nah, *I love your body in the least creepy way possible* ♥ I got myself a real thick, pudgy body, but that's just more of me to love! Sometimes it feels a little odd to love yourself and to love your body, and that's okay! Bodies suck sometimes, but that body hosts a *wonderful thing.* (it's you) (you're the wonderful thing) (you are pretty cool) Loving your own body is hard, and it doesn't make it any easier when you feel like it doesn't belong to you. But that's the body you got as of now, and you are rocking it!

Voice Dysphoria ─────────────────────

Is that my voice? Is that *my* voice?

I had really bad voice dysphoria when I first came out because my voice was kind of high-ish... But do you know who else has a high-ish voice? That's right. Any person who has been socked in the nuts. So that's okay. And if your voice is a little low? You know who has a real low voice? Ladies with them real cool voices that when they talk leave all those around who hear them shaking in their boots. You rock that voice, my pal.

What if my voice was dramatically the opposite?

If you wanted a much lower voice, just imagine if it were ridiculously low...Like, your voice on sulfur hexafluoride. That's very deep and terrifying. But what if that's how you got to sound all the time? That's pretty wicked. If you wanted a much higher voice, imagine if it were higher than Snoop Dogg on 4/20... Have you ever heard someone's voice on helium? Imagine that, *but even higher*. If you talked like that all the time, that would be pretty wild. Think if you talked the way that one singer with that super high voice sang. Again, that's pretty swanky.

Sometimes talking is hard, some people don't talk at all, and that's pretty cool!

If your voice dysphoria is incredibly awful, take a minute to think about how there are people who don't or can't talk. Imagine living in their situation if you aren't already. Maybe learn to sign and expand your communication skills without having to hear the voice that you may dislike.

I love the sound of [certain person]'s voice... what if I sounded like that?

That would be weird. Just to talk like, say, a friend or *celebrity*, even. In the same tone. Just like them. All the time. Wow.

These vocal cords are made for screaming into the void and that's just what they'll do. Join me in a shout... AHHHHHHHHHHHHHHHHHH! That was excellently refreshing. Thank you for joining me.

So those were my simple and strange ways that I get over my dysphoria. Yeah, some of them are quite silly, or ridiculous, but I find that if you can laugh at yourself, it won't bother you as much if other people laugh at you. I have been in some not-so-great situations in which people have used my dislike of myself against me to upset me, but now it's almost like I can make fun of myself too, in a way that doesn't make me upset anymore. It's hard to build resistance to rude people, but unfortunately, they aren't gonna disappear. I wish I could wave a wand and make people suck a lot less, but that's just how we are. Some of us are super great in some ways, and some of us are super terrible in other ways. We are all human, and this doesn't excuse us from our mistakes, but it doesn't mean we are irreparable. I believe in giving everyone kindness *(I'm still working on giving it to everyone, but I hold a special place in my heart for nasty people. I want to kick my foot so far up their ass that they'll be pulling toes out of their teeth for years)*, and until someone proves they are not deserving of kindness, I will simply keep talking to them with kind words, and mild passive aggression :)

Disproportionate

SAMUEL BUSCH, age 17

I feel disproportionate. The way a preteen is, like I was supposed to fill out this boy/femme body some time ago. My strange muscular thighs and semi-toned calves, full hips and short body. In short, I wish I would just be twinkie or otterish. Which is to say, tiny and thin or average height and stocky. But here I am, chunky hips, short legs and, so I've been told, a pretty face.

Several people have told me that I'm intimidating. Which makes no sense to a five-foot-two-inch tiny dude who was socialized female. Oh, and being told that my attractiveness is intimidating. Not only do I feel like a squishy little teddy bear. But the one that stays inside even after hibernation is over, saying, "Hey, yeah, I don't really want to come out right now. Like, I haven't shaved in a while."

Nobody cares what you look like; they're all thinking about themselves. "Yeah, okay, that sounds about right. I guess it's time, huh?"

Spring is here, and she's waiting for me to grow, to step out of this dark space or just open the curtains. Maybe I haven't been trying hard enough to get a bigger shoe size or sharper jawline or longer legs. Maybe she's just been waiting for me to see if I'd make the first move. She sits back, kissing two lips and inviting chrysanthemums to book and wine clubs or picnics on Sundays in the backyard. She spent weekends like me, wrapped up in snow-white blankets, suffocating under the cold, only to blossom and bloom from the pressure, and find I had new colors I didn't know of. We'd swaddle ourselves in each other, spring and fall, rebirth and death. Both new beginnings. Rain, showers and seeds falling in sun. Cool sun. Not the boiling kind that forces us out of winter skins, but nurturing and soft.

I'll hold her. As little spoon as I am, I'll hold her. Growth, death, into new; scattering of seeds and all. She makes me pure again and reminds me small things are still whole, mustard seed still persists, tiny as it is, as minuscule, it's still whole and complete.

And so am I. I am whole; small, misshapen in ways, but inherently good.

The atom makes up almost everything. No, everything. And it's one of the smallest things we can fathom. I may see my body as unattractive and thus useless but it can lift my sister. It carries the dog's food from the car and helps my mom with everything she needs. It helps my dog up the stairs, my lumpy eleven-year-old bear-sized lab, misshapen but perfect. The first love of my life, this fatty, cyst-covered furball.

So maybe my rolls and lumps are okay. If I can love him the way I do, people will love me too.

Life Journey 1
MAISIE BODRUG, age 13

These two pieces represent the complexity of life
and the confusion of puberty.

Life Journey 2

MAISIE BODRUG, age 13

Pay attention to how your trans or nonbinary friends and classmates describe their bodies and identities. Try to remember the words they use to describe themselves, and make sure you use the same words they do when you talk to or about them. It can mean a lot to your trans friends and classmates to know that someone gets them and someone cares.

—Dr. Jake Pyne

What Can I Do Now?

DR. JAKE PYNE, assistant professor in the York University School of Social Work

1. **Think about why trans freedom and equality matter to you.** Why do you think it's important to support trans people and fight for their rights? How do trans rights relate to anti-racism, to respecting Indigenous rights, to disability justice and to feminism? It's good to help other people, but part of helping is knowing why these struggles are important to all of us. Is there an experience in your own life that helps you to be an *ally*?

2. **Challenge transphobia when you hear it, as long as it is safe to do so.** Try saying something like, "Why do you think it's okay to say that?" Ask transphobic people to explain themselves, instead of always trying to explain to them why it's wrong. Check in with trans friends and class-mates about what they need when they face transphobic statements about their bodies or identities.

3. **Recognize and use your privilege to become an ally.** If you are not trans yourself, try to notice the way your body is assumed to be normal and is treated with more respect than trans bodies are. If it is safe to do so, challenge the policies in your schools and clubs if they suggest that non-trans (cis) bodies deserve better treatment—for example, access to washrooms and change rooms. Pay extra attention to how Indigenous trans youth or trans youth of color might be treated.

4. **Be a support person.** Being a supportive friend to the trans people in your life is important, and that includes accepting the negative feelings they might sometimes have about their bodies. But people might need additional help at times, beyond what you can personally do. Seek help from a trusted adult if you are worried that a young trans person you know is being mistreated at home or at school, or if they are at risk of harming themselves.

5. **Listen to trans people and change the words you use if needed.** Pay attention to how your trans or nonbinary friends and classmates describe their bodies and identities. Try to remember the words they use to describe themselves, and make sure you use the same words they do when you talk to or about them. It can mean a lot to your trans friends and classmates to know that someone gets them and someone cares.

What Can I Read Next?

PICTURE BOOKS

Pessin-Whedbee, Brook. *Who Are You? The Kid's Guide to Gender Identity.* London, UK: Jessica Kingsley Publishers, 2016.

Silverberg, Cory. *What Makes a Baby.* New York, NY: Seven Stories Press, 2012. *Also available in French*

YA AND GRAPHIC NOVELS

Labelle, Sophie. *Sex Ed for Everyone: Comics about Relationships, Identities and Puberty.* Montreal, QC: Serious Trans Vibes, 2019. *Also available in French*

Simon, Rachel E. *The Every Body Book: The LGBTQ+ Inclusive Guide for Kids about Sex, Gender, Bodies, and Families.* London, UK: Jessica Kingsley Publishers, 2020.

GENERAL AUDIENCE

Gonzales, Kathryn, and Karen Rayne. *Trans+: Love, Sex, Romance, and Being You.* Washington, DC: Magination Press, 2019.

Sharman, Zena, ed. *The Remedy: Queer and Trans Voices on Health and Health Care.* Vancouver, BC: Arsenal Pulp Press, 2016.

MEMOIRS/FIRST-PERSON NARRATIVES

Johnson, George M. *All Boys Aren't Blue: A Memoir-Manifesto.* New York, NY: Farrar Straus Giroux Books for Young Readers, 2020.

Kergil, Skylar. *Before I Had Words: On Being a Transgender Young Adult.* New York, NY: Skyhorse Publishing, 2017.

Symington, Sabrina. *First Year Out: A Transition Story.* London, UK: Singing Dragon, 2018.

Government Buildings

AJAM, age 14

Everyday Life

What everyday activities, such as traveling, using social media or practicing your faith, are more difficult or complicated because of who you are?

What everyday activities in your life might be different if your gender expression changed?

How are everyday spaces and things, like washrooms and ID cards, designed to reinforce the gender binary? How could you reimagine them as more inclusive?

Hidden Transphobia

TOR BROUGHTON, age 12

"They/them is plural though," he says.

"No it's not! You're being transphobic!" I viciously reply.

"That's not transphobic!" I hear that lie echo in my ears all too often. Whether it's people who truly believe they aren't doing anything wrong or people who are just flat-out bad, we need to pay more attention to these things.

People tend to subconsciously be racist, sexist, trans-phobic, **homophobic** or discriminatory without even noticing. It's human nature to try and judge people based on looks when we first see them; it's a survival skill. We look and judge to see if someone's a threat. It's not in human nature to discriminate against someone. People are oblivious to their bad actions. We are taught to hate. We are taught to discriminate. It's not natural to verbally or physically hate on someone due to gender, race, sexuality, social class or any other difference.

You can be posting all the posts you want about "I love trans people," but if your love doesn't include people of color, obese people, men and women who are tall, short, weak, strong, autistic, broke, depressed, non-Christian, disabled, nonbinary, questioning, it's not real love. If your feminism is based off of the uterus and not off women, it's not real feminism. Include trans people!

I understand if it's against your religious morals or beliefs to be LGBTQ+. But that doesn't mean you suddenly have the power to discriminate. You might think that what you're saying isn't hurtful or transphobic/trans ignorant. But if a trans person tells you that it is, it is. You do not have the power to decide if you're being transphobic. Also, just because you are LGB or **BIPOC** or a woman or any other minority, that doesn't make you immune to being transphobic. If someone transgender or a nonbinary person tells you that you're being transphobic, you are, end of story.

Simply put, watch what you're saying and look out for others. Respect people's differences and be kind. Listen to them when they tell you that you're being discriminatory and then change! When life is unfair, you don't have to be.

Airport

JASPER LEDGERWOOD, age 14

I am in an airport, and I am afraid.

I'm fourteen years old.
It's only my third time traveling alone.
This should be what scares me,
But it's not.

46% of people hate me for who I am.
20% hate me for who I love.

Is it the middle-aged man
Reading the newspaper in the seat next to me?

Is it the exhausted mother,
Two kids in tow?

I am in an airport, and I am afraid.

Someone like me is murdered every 31 hours.
I have to be on my guard,
Carefully calculate everything I do.
I already have a target on my back.
Don't want to make it worse.

My life is like a game of roulette.

Am I next?

Am I doing enough to ensure my parents won't get a call

Telling them their kid won't be coming home?

Which bathroom can I use without drawing attention to myself?

Will I even reach adulthood?

I am in an airport, and I am afraid.

**46% of people hate me for who I am.
20% hate me for who I love.**

—Jasper Ledgerwood

They're right about one thing: I am not simple. At best, I am a question that begs asking; at worst, I am the brick that toppled their masterpiece.

—*Christopher*

The Plan

CHRISTOPHER, age 17

I'm not religious, but you could call me a romantic in that I like to think this world has a plan. Out there somewhere, I trust in a blueprint, and from primordial ooze to the inevitable, sun-scorched grave, every base on this planet seems to be covered. Except one.

As it turns out, the plan has no place for me. That's what they've hammered into me since the day I learned my own name: I am the mutation, the broken puzzle piece, the fatal detour off the straight and narrow. When they tell me I shouldn't exist, I sputter, as anyone would—but then I begin to panic. My alarm bells ring, not because they say it, but because for a moment I believe them.

And so the search begins. Before their accusations can settle, I'm scouring, frantic, for my rebuttal—some kind of secret code, written into the earth itself, that will wave a steady hand and tell them, "Don't worry. He is as natural as you are." I trust only experts, so I turn to those wardens of the world who pre-date our petty arguments, and hope they'll point me toward an age-old precedent for lives like mine. They should know, after all. They are the animals, they are the plants, and they are the stars.

Unfortunately, they're also cryptic bastards, and I find no easy answer. Penguins fall in love, the earth reshapes itself and stars explode, but girls do not turn into boys. If I squint hard enough, I might see traces of myself in mysterious fish and poisonous frogs that transform from one thing to another. I might pretend that I, too, am a courageous pioneer of evolution, elaborately constructed to push the species forth. But no ancient animal has ever been so contentious, and unlike the rest of them, I did not strategize this. I am a fluke, a dent in nature's rules. Maybe I'm all the things people say about me. Impractical. Haphazard. Absurd.

Either way, they're right about one thing: I am not simple. At best, I am a question that begs asking; at worst, I am the brick that toppled their masterpiece. When I see it through their eyes, I realize they're mourning not just a convention of biology, but something sacred, something they could understand without effort and trust without risk. They found comfort in simplicity—simple men, simple women—and I cut it to swathes.

So I forgive them for calling me broken, and stupid, and unnatural. It was only their attempt to make sense of things. In time, I forgive myself, too, for breaking the heirloom the universe gave them. I learn to accept my title as the one who made things complicated, who strayed from the earth's tradition and stumbled into territory that is uniquely human.

And I wonder if I'm going crazy or if the world just delivered my answer.

Because the truth is, we are not the animals, and we are not the plants, and we are not the stars. We are human beings, and maybe the simplest thing about us is that we defy every rule we write. We are so desperate for a cure to our own natural chaos that we look for it in all the wrong places, and try to force answers where questions should be. It's a strange kind of masochism, our attempts to explain ourselves. No one knows it better than I do.

But in the absence of answers, I have found the only thing that makes sense. I do not follow the rules of the rest of the world, but I follow the rules of being human. Hidden between the lines of code in this universe is the verdict, plain and simple, that not all things are meant to be so easily understood.

Something tells me that was part of the plan all along.

Tools of the Transgender Teen

TOR BROUGHTON, age 12

Being trans is neat
Except when people are mean
Why can't we be kind
Binders, Lupron, T
Tools of the transgender teen
Keeping us alive
That is why we need to be kind

Why is it us
   the bullied ones who rise to new heights when all is lost
Why is it us the abused ones who stand up for the survivors
Why is it us
   the misunderstood ones who listen to crazy ideas when others can not
Why is it us the hated ones that will love when strong ones won't
Why is it us
   the feared ones that will show others not t fear when others refuse

Alexander

Queer, But Still a Christian

ALEXANDER M-G, age 13

While being *queer* and a Christian is rewarding, it is also hard, because in the queer community, most people talk about how Christians don't accept queer people, while most Christians talk about how queer people are bad. I'm caught between two worlds, and I wanted to show that in my work.

What Can I Do Now?

DR. LEE AIRTON, assistant professor of Gender and Sexuality Studies in Education at Queen's University

1. **Let trans people decide when and how they talk about their gender identity.** The things we find hurtful or frustrating are things that hurt or frustrate cis people too, like bumping our elbows, fighting a headache that won't go away, stepping in poop, getting dumped or waiting in line when we're already late. If you have a trans friend, remember that most of their life isn't about being trans. When they need to talk to you about being trans, they will, but let them take the lead. No one wants to think or be reminded about their gender all the time.

2. **Support your trans friends.** Friendships and relationships are extremely important for trans youth. Your trans friends are counting on you to be there for them, even if in the most ordinary ways ever, like checking in or playing a game or sharing a cat video. We might not ask for this enough, but you can be sure we need it.

3. **Remember that being trans is unique to each trans person.** There are many things that trans guys share, many things trans girls experience in a similar way, and lots of things nonbinary youth have in common. So if you have a trans friend whose gender or needs around it don't make sense to you, or that are different from what you already know about trans people, don't send a message that they are from outer space. Imagine what it feels like when you are telling a story and someone really, truly, believes you. Think about what their face, body and voice are doing, and try your best to show your friend that you believe them too.

4. **Ask for all-gender washrooms.** If you spend time in a community center, after-school program, coffee shop, arcade or gym, see if you can find an all-gender washroom or change room. If you can't, ask staff where they are and explain why this matters—that some trans people are nonbinary and don't use gendered facilities, and that having a private option can be safer for many people. You can even make up a nonbinary friend to ask about if you don't have one already. "My friend is nonbinary and wants to come with me to this program next time, but I'm worried they won't have anywhere to pee." You'll be helping adults get ready for when nonbinary youth *do* show up. And they will!

5. **Use *they*.** Young people are generally more comfortable than adults saying "they are" for one person. People who study language tell us this is because you actually speak a different English than your parents or guardians (whoa!). But you still might feel awkward, which is okay. So practice. When gender doesn't matter and you're telling a story or talking about someone, say "they are" instead of "he is" or "she is." Who cares who sold you the pizza slice, as long as it's hot? If it isn't, say, "*They* gave me a cold slice. WTF?" Then go get your needs met.

> **When gender doesn't matter and you're telling a story or talking about someone, say "they are" instead of "he is" or "she is." Who cares who sold you the pizza slice, as long as it's hot? If it isn't, say, "*They* gave me a cold slice."**
>
> —*Dr. Lee Airton*

What Can I Read Next?

PICTURE BOOKS

Adeyoha, Koja, and Angel Adeyoha. *47,000 Beads*. Toronto, ON: Flamingo Rampant, 2017.

Roher, Megan. *Transgender Children of God*. San Francisco, CA: Wilgefortis Press, 2016.

YA AND GRAPHIC NOVELS

Bongiovanni, Archie, and Tristan Jimerson. *A Quick & Easy Guide to They/Them Pronouns*. Portland, OR: Limerence Press, 2018.

Fisher, Owl, and Fox Fisher. *Trans Teen Survival Guide*. London, UK: Jessica Kingsley Publishers, 2019.

Nicholson, Hope. *Love Beyond Body, Space and Time: An Indigenous LGBT Sci-Fi Anthology*. Winnipeg, MB: Bedside Press, 2016.

GENERAL AUDIENCE

Airton, Lee. *Gender: Your Guide; A Gender-Friendly Primer on What to Know, What to Say, and What to Do in the New Gender Culture*. Avon, MA: Adams Media, 2018.

Hartke, Austen. *Transforming: The Bible & the Lives of Transgender Christians*. Louisville, KY: Westminster John Knox Press, 2018.

MEMOIRS/FIRST-PERSON NARRATIVES

Belcourt, Billy-Ray. *This Wound Is a World*. Minneapolis, MN: University of Minnesota Press, 2019.

Also available in French.

Stein, Abby Chava. *Becoming Eve: My Journey from Ultra-Orthodox Rabbi to Transgender Woman*. Seattle, WA: Seal Press, 2019.

Where Do We Draw the Dividing Line?

AJAM, age 14

Schools

When you witness
or experience
bullying, how
is that bullying
gendered?

How does the gender
segregation of certain school
activities pose barriers for
trans kids? For all kids?

How do teachers
and schools either
encourage or prevent
transphobia in schools?

A Couple of Days in the Life of One Trans Person

MAISIE BODRUG, age 13

My boobs are made of silicone
(I sometimes forget to put them on).
Forget them one day and poof! They're gone.

When I'm at school, I'm kinda stealth
(and take vitamin D for my health).
You call me a freak, I'll call you a fool.
Just 'cause I'm unique doesn't mean I'm not cool.

When it's time for bed, I remove my boobs and shout,
"I am awesome!"
Then I hit the lights out.

I wake up in the morning, I rub my eyes and yawn,
Walk up to the bedside table, turn the lamp on.
My mom calls up, "It's breakfast!" and I say "Just a minute!"
She made me an omelet; I wonder what's in it.

I finish up my breakfast, and I go and pack my bag,
Then run into a bigot. He starts calling me a fag.
I go and confront him—I say, "Leave me alone."
He tells me that I'm garbage and that he sits on the throne!
I tell him, "That does it." I'm boiling with rage.
I tell him he's a douchebag and that he should act his age.

I get to class and take my seat; we're doing science!
It's gonna be sweet!
We're studying hormones! What a surprise!
Estrogen! Testosterone! I can't believe my eyes!
I go to lunch—it's a burger and fries!
Then someone calls me a tranny and part of me dies.

**My boobs are made of silicone
(I sometimes forget to put them on).
Forget them one day and
poof! They're gone.**

—*Maisie Bodrug*

I don't want to be afraid to go to school. I don't want to have to tear down signs and notes stuck on my locker. I don't want to have to wear my headphones while I walk in the halls so I don't have to hear the things these kids say about me...

—*Anonymous*

Student Letter Responding to the Backlash on the Sexual Orientation and Gender Identity (SOGI) Curriculum

ANONYMOUS, a trans student between the age of 14 and 17

I don't want to be afraid to go to school. I don't want to have to tear down signs and notes stuck on my locker. I don't want to have to wear my headphones while I walk in the halls so I don't have to hear the things these kids say about me...

You say that you don't want the school experience to be ruined for your kids with teaching of SOGI, but my school experience has been forever tainted by the unkind things said and done by *those* kids. They tell me that a man I don't even know hates me, and that I'm going to hell for being who I am; they tell me that I am disgusting and a disgrace. There are so many other words that they've said to me that have become ingrained in my mind so deeply that I was convinced I didn't even deserve to be alive. The number of days I lie in bed terrified to go to school far outweigh the number of days that I'm not.

Do you know how it feels to be afraid to walk down the hallways, terrified that everyone around you is talking about you behind your back? To be terrified that someone might hurt you or shout at you? Do you know how it feels to walk up to your locker and see words scrawled across it, and papers pasted to it with words that hurt more than any punch ever could? Every single day, I am terrified to go to school, to go to a place built on learning and love but that's filled with hatred. I'm terrified to check my social media ever since someone posted a picture of me with a noose drawn around my neck. I'm terrified to live.

If students knew that I am no different than they are, maybe I wouldn't have to be so terrified. Maybe I would be able to live my life carefree, like I did when I was a young child. If we could teach at a young age that being transgender, or being queer in general, is okay, maybe I wouldn't have lost as many friends as I have. If we could teach children that it is okay to be themselves, think of how much happier they could be. When I was 10 years old and said that I liked people of the same gender, I had two different responses from the people around me. They were either indifferent, or they were violently grossed out and were quick to judge. I wish they didn't care. I wish I never had to hear people telling me "that's not what God intended," or "that's a sin," or "that's gross."

I was a young kid—no, I was a *child.*

People say that we are pushing our "agenda" onto kids, yet we see babies and toddlers wearing clothing with slogans like "ladies' man" and "chick magnet" amongst many others, so it begs the question, Whose alleged "agenda" is being forced on whom? We don't have an *agenda.* We just want to educate kids and teens to make them understand that it's okay to be "different." I wish that this was part of the curriculum when I was younger. I wish that I could have said, "Yes, I am transgender" without people asking me what "turned me" this way, or what "made me feel like" I had to be this way. Nothing made me *want* to be trans, nothing *made me* want to be "different," I just wanted to be *me* and wanted to be accepted.

I'm lucky because I have family who support me. I'm lucky because I at least still have some friends who weren't appalled by my existence. Some kids aren't. I've lost friends who weren't accepted by their families and peers to suicide. These deaths weren't because they weren't brave enough or strong enough, like some may say. It was because they had to fight every day and they were in a place that they could not win. They were beaten and bruised with words and fists and notes. They were disrespected and harassed by people around them, and this group has the audacity to say that they don't tolerate hate? How dare you. How dare you let these kids suffer and lead themselves to destruction because you don't want your children to know that they exist. How dare you say that you won't tolerate hate when it is the same people who attack me and my friends. How dare you say that you want what is best for the kids when the only kids you care about are the "normal" ones.

My teachers, counselors and the other staff at my school... they have done so much to support me, they have done so much to be inclusive and to be respectful of *all* students. We aren't asking for "special rights." We are just asking to be acknowledged and respected. We aren't asking for "more." We are asking for the same respect that all students deserve. We're asking to be treated like *people*. That's all I want. I just want to be treated like a *person*.

My teacher asks me why I'm not
handing in my schoolwork
And why when I could be skipping
grades, I'm skipping classes.
I felt insane,
So I assumed I was.

— *Owen Miller*

When You Call Me "She"

OWEN MILLER, age 16

When you speak with someone who thinks you're someone
you're not,
You begin to feel every word is a lie.

Every sound over my lips feels lipstick-stained.
It feels like dead girl's blood is smeared across my mouth.
It drips over the apple at my throat and dries like wax.
It stings when I try to scrape it off: it yanks the hair from my skin.

When someone calls me "she,"
It's grade four again, and my world is upside down.
I'm peeling duct tape off my calf with one hand,
The other sticking to the cold pole by the sweat on my palm.
I'm struggling to keep the blood from rushing to my head,
Struggling to keep the name that isn't mine out of my mind,
But they force it through my ears like claps of thunder.
Stones hail my body and their echoes crack the asphalt.
My bare, innocent skin swirls into a storm of red, orange, blue
and purple.
Raindrops glide off my jaw and paint the daisies red.
When someone calls me "she,"
I hear it again:
"Freak." "Tranny." "Dyke."

When you call me "she,"
I'm in grade eight again.
I'm sitting in an empty bathtub, the hairs on my neck raised.
The humid air around me seems to vibrate,
Settling on the curve of my shoulders and hips, hair sticking
to my clammy skin.
Rich red streams gush down my forearm and scarlet tendrils
dribble into my trembling palm,
Their deathly fingertips struggling to intertwine with mine.
I live in a hazy world that barely feels real, even under the
light of dusk.
I try to dig past this foreign skin
And find relief in the realization that I am nothing but blood,
skin, bones.
I'm bound to no expectations, none of your creations.
Sunlight makes my head spin and my stomach churn.
My teacher asks me why I'm not handing in my schoolwork
And why when I could be skipping grades, I'm skipping
classes.
I felt insane,
So I assumed I was.

When you call me "she,"
You're talking past me.
Though I know you have no malicious intent,
I see sun-kissed skin setting to ash,
Droplets on my water bottle slipping into bloody rivulets
down the drain,

Musty mildew asphyxiating brisk dawn airways.
You're making a game out of fight or flight:
My heartbeat slams adrenaline through my veins at the
thought of going back to that place.

It's grade ten.
I'm learning to speak
As none other than myself
Through chest-hollowing gasps,
White fire locked under my tongue,
Frustration bubbling like bile in my throat.
I accept that I'm no "she,"
Struggle against their animosity,
And choke back the shame.

Four years reborn and I've never wanted to kill myself.
The most anxiety I get is worrying about exam marks
Until you call me "she."
So yes, my pronoun is a big deal to me,
And it's not okay when you don't use it.

Being transgender isn't a mental illness;
The denial of someone's right to identity is.

When I came across *nonbinary*, it felt like something clicked inside me and I finally understood why I had felt so out of place for so long. All of a sudden, I was a part of something so unique and wonderful while also finding a piece of my identity jigsaw.

—Luna

Boy or Girl?

LUNA, age 14

I shuffle toward my closet and sigh. "Here we go again," I mumble. One by one, I push every shirt I have to the side until I find my favorite flannel. Gray, just like my mood. I plop a black beanie on my head and I'm ready to go. I try to wear dark clothing to hide what my mom always calls "the beautiful curves that God gave me." She thinks that I need to start to embrace the body that I was given, but really, what good is that going to do if it's the wrong one? I don't tell her this, of course, because I would just get the same response I always do.

"You are perfect just the way you are. You were given the body you have for a reason."

Now, my mom is a wonderful woman, don't get me wrong, but (a) I am not about to start "embracing myself" for her and (b) I'm not out to her yet. She just doesn't understand. Which is why I haven't come out in the first place. Trying to help her understand would be insurmountable. I found the label *nonbinary* sometime last year when I was scouting online for internet friends. There were a bunch of accounts that I found where people would put their sexual orientations and gender identities in their bios. At that time, I had no idea that gender identities other than the binary existed.

When I came across *nonbinary*, it felt like something clicked inside me and I finally understood why I had felt so out of place for so long. All of a sudden, I was a part of something so unique and wonderful while also finding a piece of my identity jigsaw.

A vibration in my back pocket interrupts my thoughts. It's a text from my best friend, Isabella.

Morning Georgia ☺

My heart sinks. I'm not out to anyone except for my online friends. I want to come out to Isabella, but I just don't think she'll understand. We've been best friends since we were really little, and even though I am very tomboyish, as she would say, she knows me as a girl and wouldn't be able to see me otherwise. I'm going to have to say something soon, though. I can't stand not being able to tell her the truth.

Morning Bella.

Did you hear that Charlie is actually a boy now? I ask, testing the water.

Yeah! It's so awesome and brave of him! I'm happy that he can finally express himself like he wants to.

Whew! That went way better than I thought it would. Maybe coming out won't be as hard as I thought.

"I know right?! anyway I'll see you at school.

Hope lights up inside me. "I can do this," I whisper to myself. "One person at a time." I sling my backpack over my shoulder and grab a waffle off the kitchen counter. "Bye, Mom!" I yell from the front door.

"Goodbye! Have a nice day, sweetheart!"

The walk to my school isn't that far, so I'm always early. The chilly November wind on top of the overcast sky makes the schoolyard look especially deserted today. When I'm out to everyone, I want to start going by the name Grey because it reminds me of these kinds of days. Overcast skies may seem kind of yucky to most, but I love them. They mean that rain is on its way, and rain is spectacular.

As I am unlocking my locker, I hear a snicker from behind me. I turn around to find three girls that I used to be friends with chuckling and pointing at me. Ashley, Mackenzie and Justice are always harassing someone. I take things really personally, so I'm the most fun to pick on.

"What are you even wearing?" says Ashley, wearing a cruel grin.

"Flannels are for dykes," adds Justice venomously.

I feel my face go bright red. I grab my books and slam my locker door, turn quickly in the opposite direction and speed-walk down the hallway, straight into the bathroom. Luckily, it's empty. Looking at myself in the mirror, I immediately regret picking out this shirt, even though it's my favorite. In a stall I take it off and throw on a baggy hoodie that hides the things I don't like. No matter how hard I try, the stupid things those girls say to me still bother me. They pick on everything that I hate, as if my self-esteem isn't low enough already.

Back in the hallway Bella comes up behind me and jumps on my back. "Hey, G!"

"Hello, Bella," I say back with a smile. She always brightens my day.

"Look, there's Charlie!" Isabella nods in his direction.

"Yeah. He's pretty great. I'm kinda envious of his bravery."

Isabella gets off my back and starts walking beside me. "Me too! He's just so proud to be himself, and nothing anyone says brings him down. He's kind of my school idol."

This is a very good thing.

"What do you think about transgender people?" I ask, timid.

She smiles widely at me. "I think that they are very bold and should be able to be whoever they want to be without any repercussions. Anyway, I have English—maybe we can talk more at lunch?"

I nod eagerly and feel butterflies spring to life in my belly. "See you then!"

10:42. The clock could not possibly go any slower. 10:56. My Humanities teacher is droning on and on about Galileo and I cannot stop thinking about what to say to Bella. Finally, at 11:05, the bell rings and I hop up from my seat and bound out the door, into the crowded artery of a hallway.

Meet me in the caf? I text Bella. She quickly responds with a thumbs-up.

On my way to the cafeteria I decide to take a pit stop in the bathroom. Bad idea. Two girls jump as I enter and giggle.

"You're in the wrong bathroom! The boys' washroom is around the corner."

I laugh along with them and dart back into the hallway. I'll just hold it until I get home.

Isabella is waiting in line to buy a wrap for lunch. "Hey," I whisper in her ear, sneaking up on her.

"Jeez, you scared me half to death!" she says, holding a hand over her heart. "How was class?"

"Boring as usual." I roll my eyes. "How was your class?"

She shrugs. "You know I love English, but we are doing some dull novel study and I just want to do poetry."

I laugh. "You are such a nerd."

She grins widely at me. "I take pride in it. Now, what were we talking about before school?"

Yes! This is what I've been waiting for. "Charlie. And then we were talking about transgender people," I say.

"Oh yes. I think that they are awesome!" She pays for her wrap and we head to our small little corner of the cafeteria that we've unofficially claimed.

"Me too. Have you heard of other gender identities, like nonbinary, for example?"

She tilts her head ever so slightly, thinking, and then says, "I've heard of it, but I'm not quite sure what it means."

Well, at least she's heard of it.

"It's pretty much an umbrella term for people who identify with genders that are not exclusively masculine or feminine or genders outside of the binary."

Isabella's eyes widen and she puts her hand up. "Wait, hold on. There are more genders?" she says, already confused.

This might take awhile. By the end of lunch, I think she has somewhat of an idea of what I'm talking about when I use the term *nonbinary*. Personally, I believe we've made great progress.

"So why are you telling me all this stuff, G?" Isabella asks me as we walk to Biology.

I feel my whole body start to shake. I take a tentative glance toward Bella, who is smiling at me patiently.

"I, uh, well, I kind of think I am nonbinary, I guess," I mumble as I become very fascinated with a scuff on the white tip of my Converse.

"Are you kidding?" she says, looking at me with wide eyes.

"No?" I say, getting progressively more anxious.

"No, I mean, that's super awesome!!!" Bella smiles excitedly and hops around a little. "See? You are already cool and now you are even cooler! Why do you look so nervous?"

"I just had no idea that you would take this so well! I'll see you after school, okay?"

She nods and skips down the hallway to her last class. I can't help but smile like an idiot the rest of the day.

"So can you explain more about this stuff to me? Like how it relates to you, I mean?" Bella asks as we walk to my house. She comes over almost every day.

"Of course. I guess I can start off by saying that I personally identify as neither man nor woman but somewhere in between, whereas some others who identify with the term nonbinary may identify as more masculine, more feminine or maybe something completely separate."

She nods slowly. "So it doesn't matter what sex you were assigned at birth?"

"No. It's more about how you feel about your gender inside."

"That makes sense."

I smile softly and walk very lightly the rest of the way home. Just when we are about to reach the front door, she breaks the peaceful silence.

"Well, what do I call you?"

I quickly open the door and rush Isabella upstairs to my bedroom, closing the door quietly.

"Well, you are the first person I've told all this, so you can't call me anything aloud yet, but I've always wanted my name to be Grey." I look at my feet, embarrassed.

"That's a great name for you, G," she says with a loving smile. "You know that I will always love you, no matter your gender or who you fall in love with or whatever. I'll always be here for you, okay?"

I look up at Bella, who is smiling softly as she pulls me into a hug. "Okay, Bella. I love you. Thank you so much for being my best friend."

"I love you too, G. Always." We hug for a while and then do our homework together.

After she's left, my mom comes up to my bedroom door and knocks three times. "Hey, can I come in?" she says softly.

"Yeah, sure." The door creaks as she pushes it open slowly. I swivel around in my desk chair to face her. She sits on the end of my bed and looks around my room for a few seconds before looking at me.

"I, uh, heard what you and Isabella were talking about, and I just want you to know that you can be whoever you want to be and I will still love you. I will never stop loving you or hold who you are or who you love against you." She smiles lovingly.

"Thanks, Mom. I'm sorry that you found all this stuff out this way instead of me telling you directly, but if you ever have questions, I'm here. I really appreciate you telling me this."

"Of course. I'm your mom!" She rises from my bed and flattens the sheets where she was sitting. Standing in the doorway, she says, "We're having spaghetti for dinner. It should be done in about 10 minutes. Come down when you are ready." She strides out of the room and closes the door behind her.

So, I think to myself, even though there are some horrible people that do horrible things and some people who will never accept people like me, if I focus on all of the wonderful and accepting people in my life, maybe all this won't be as hard.

Strength

FINN LEWIS, age 13

The art piece is meant to express feelings about being transgender in some rough school surroundings. The rainbow-colored head in the air is the part of my character that expresses my feelings of creativity. The clouds are the city I've created.

What Can I Do Now?

LINDSAY CAVANAUGH, full-time PhD student at the Ontario Institute for Studies in Education at the University of Toronto

1. **Remember that trans students, educators and parents/guardians are already in schools!** If you don't know them, they probably don't feel terribly safe being visible. Start asking yourself what supports and resources exist at your school. For example, does your school have a club for queer and trans students (commonly referred to as a GSA)? Does your school have an all-gender washroom?

2. **Be proactive.** Ask for multi-stall, all-gender washrooms, or request trans-related books in the school library. Don't wait for trans students, teachers or families to out themselves as a way of advocating for changes in a school.

3. **Apologize and move on.** Be open and respectful when a friend or classmate tells you they use a different pronoun than what you expect. Start using that pronoun, and when you make a mistake, don't make a big deal out of it. Apologize, keep trying and move on.

4. **When playing at recess, outside or in the gym, make sure your sports and activities are open and inclusive of all genders.** Boys don't have to play certain games and girls other ones. Remember that some people do not align with the gender binary, and you might not know someone's gender identity by looking at them. No one should have to out themselves to join the fun. Make all your sports and PE activities welcoming to all gender identities and expressions.

5. **Remember that trans people are more than just trans.** Read and learn from Two-Spirit people, trans people of color, *neurodiverse* trans folks and trans people with disabilities and chronic illnesses. Trans people have so many different identities and experiences. There is no single trans story.

Trans people have so many different
identities and experiences.
There is no single trans story.

—*Lindsay Cavanaugh*

What Can I Read Next?

PICTURE BOOKS

Baldacchino, Christine. *Morris Micklewhite and the Tangerine Dress*. Toronto, ON: Groundwood Books, 2014.

Moradian, Afsaneh. *Jamie Is Jamie: A Book about Being Yourself and Playing Your Way*. Minneapolis, MN: Free Spirit Publishing, 2018.

Thom, Kai Cheng. *From the Stars in the Sky to the Fish in the Sea*. Vancouver, BC: Arsenal Pulp Press, 2017. *Also available in French*

YA AND GRAPHIC NOVELS

Callender, Kacen. *Felix Ever After*. New York, NY: Balzer & Bray/Harperteen, 2020.

Williamson, Lisa. *The Art of Being Normal*. Oxford, UK: David Fickling Books, 2020. *Also available in French*

GENERAL AUDIENCE

Jiménez, Karleen Pendeleton. *Tomboys and Other Gender Heroes: Confessions from the Classroom*. New York, NY: Peter Lang Publishing, 2016.

Killermann, Sam. *A Guide to Gender: The Social Justice Advocate's Handbook*, 2nd ed. Austin, TX: Impetus Books, 2017.

Woolley, Susan W., and Lee Airton. *Teaching about Gender Diversity: Teacher-Tested Lesson Plans for K-12 Classrooms*. Toronto, ON: Canadian Scholars Press, 2020.

MEMOIRS/FIRST-PERSON NARRATIVES

Rajunov, Micah, and Scott Duane. *Nonbinary: Memoirs of Gender and Identity*. New York, NY: University of Columbia Press, 2019.

Spoon, Rae, & Ivan Coyote. *Gender Failure*. Vancouver, BC: Arsenal Pulp Press, 2014.

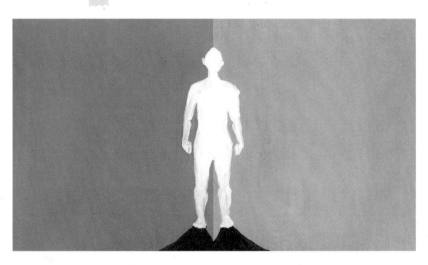

Transcend

AJAM, age 14

Mental Health

Have you or a loved one ever experienced mental illness? Did gender or gender expectations play into that unwellness?

How do the stories in this chapter show the relationship between transphobia and mental illness? What about the relationship between gender dysphoria and mental illness?

Do you notice patterns in how the trans youth in this chapter coped with their mental health struggles?

When there are really bad days when it seems impossible to do anything, just know that there is someone who exists who has been changed, in even the tiniest way, by knowing you. You, just as you are, are so important.

—A.J. Gabriel

Self-Care

A.J. GABRIEL, age 17

Because of my strange relationship with both my mental health and my identity, I have learned that I don't always understand what I'm doing in life. I have things that I will never forget, though, and these things stick with me every day that passes by. I like lists, and I like odd numbers, so of course, being who I am, I have a list of seven things that I don't want to forget, seven things that I will always remember. Some are simple reminders, some are things that have been told to me by people that are close to me and my heart. These are the little reminders for whenever I feel down and out, and I want to share them. I want people to maybe get an inside look at the mind of a queer teenager. These are feelings that I have had hard times dealing with, and they are ideas that I did not always embrace, but because I am human, and I am always changing, I have learned that these are the seven things that hold so much importance to me. They are seven things I learned when I was at a point so low that I thought I had nothing left. I had nothing but words in my head, and these are what kept me fighting for better days.

1. **You are worth it.** Simple, simple words can change the day. Maybe you don't believe that you're worth it, maybe you don't understand what you bring to the world, but you are powerful and excellent. If you don't know what you do to make the world how it is, find it. Find the purpose you have. Even if today your purpose was to just stay asleep most of the day, or just wake up and do some self-care, that's okay. Every day is different—that's what makes life unpredictable.

2. **Today is your record for the most amount of days you lived. Keep that record climbing higher.** As of the time I write this, I've been alive for over 6,000 days. I'm going for 10,000 next. I'm gonna kick my ass and beat my own record!

3. **You have beat 100 percent of your hardest days— you're doing great.** Look at you go, just winning and living it up. All those shitty and relatively *yikes* kind of days you've had—you've come out alive! Sometimes that's all you can do: survive. But hey, that means you get more days to make things different! More days to find new hobbies, meet new people, get a new pet…whatever it is that makes you feel a good feeling. You're doing amazing. I'm proud of you.

4. **There's something that's been keeping you here all this time. What is it?** Sometimes there's this feeling that nothing is worth it anymore. But you and your life are worth fighting for. You've stayed all this time when at any point you could have theoretically given up. Do you know why you're here? Do any of us know why we are where we are, or *who* we are? Find out, find yourself, find something new about yourself that you never knew.

5. **Sometimes you're lost, but you will always be found.** Maybe it won't be today, or tomorrow, or next week even. Life has a funny way of getting in the way when we don't want it to. But something huge that I've learned is that you have to find yourself where you lost yourself, and from there, rebuild yourself even stronger than before.

6. **Just because today sucked doesn't mean tomorrow is gonna be just as awful.** Life's too short to be upset about everything all the time, yet here I am, the constant wet blanket of every event I go to. But hey, guess what? That's okay! It's okay to have feelings. It is also fine to have bad days. There are going to be days when all you want to do is give up. This is 100 percent true and extremely understandable. On the flip side, there are going to be days when all you want is to keep going and keep fighting. Who knows what kind of day tomorrow will be. What will it bring? I guess the only way to find out is to stay and see.

7. **The past is the past, and the future will forever remain something to be desired.** This goes to say, things that happened in the past are just that—old news. But doesn't mean that they weren't important or impactful. They always say in sci-fi-type movies that when you go back to the past not to change a thing because it will forever drastically alter the present. But why don't we think of our lives right *now* in the same light? If every little action can have a drastic effect on our future, why stay silent? If one small thing can change the present, what can we do with our future?

———

There are trillions of planets that exist in the galaxies here and farther on. We were put on this planet for some reason, and we continue to change it every second of each day. I'm a strong believer in the butterfly effect, and I feel that everything we do comes from something else that has affected us, and further goes to affect things around us. We are here for some weird, inexplicable reason, and sometimes it feels like we don't deserve to be here, don't deserve to take up the precious oxygen that we consume, or don't deserve to take up a place in society—especially if society has tried to outcast us for years. The world doesn't stop for anyone, and maybe the thought of disappearing is so strong that you feel nothing will change without you, but that's simply not true. Just because the world doesn't stop for anyone doesn't mean that to someone, you weren't their world. When there are really bad days when it seems impossible to do anything, just know that there is someone who exists who has been changed, in even the tiniest way, by knowing you. You, just as you are, are so important.

Words and Lists

Some words have a tendency to make you feel utterly horrible, so incredibly so that you wish you could be a turtle who could retract their neck and head inside of their shell anytime someone says *moist*. This is just a fact. I, for one, happen to have a journal that I keep and write down words and sentences that make me happy. I love little things, and putting them together can make me feel less like a dumpster fire. I love lists, words, odd numbers, dogs, my hair, the concept of a clown-cowboy hybrid...but I don't always have all of those things on me when I'm upset. The things that I do have are words, and I have ones that I like to say just because they sound real nifty. Sometimes I'll just say them to myself when I'm upset or when I'm having a lot of anxiety or when I don't know how to react to a situation.

The weird thing is that these words don't really mean much to me or hold any significant value. I just like the way they sound when I say them. It's strange how a series of syllables put together can make me convince myself that I'm doing well. I'm going to leave my list of words that I like to say, and I'm gonna encourage everyone who stumbles upon this piece to do the same.

castle	rhododendron	decrepit
glass	anecdotal	chelicerates
pariah	correlate	thorn
duodenum	Saoirse	lackadaisical
corrode	juxtaposition	conundrum

When I'm having a big ol' bout of *STRESS*, I will just say these words either aloud or at least in my head. They make me feel calm, even though I only ever really say them when I am in fact *not* calm.

I Am Strong

TOR BROUGHTON, age 12

I am strong
As I look in the mirror trying to see myself
Realizing that he's not there
That's her
Victoria
That terrible word runs through my head
But I stand there telling myself who I am
I am strong
As I go to the gym and lift
I feel weak
When I see cis guys all muscular and lucky
As the pain of not being on T hits me
I keep lifting
I am strong
I get my **blocker** shot
The tears stream down into a waterfall of hopelessness
As I tell myself the shots aren't worth it
The pain I push through

I am strong

As I'm misgendered and told I'm not a real boy
While my grandparents tell me where I'm headed in the
afterlife
Hell
The word I see written across the letter they wrote me
Hell
I put it away
I am strong
The cameras, lights and mics pushed into my face
Because I thanked the prime minister
Tears run again as he speaks to me
The tears I've been told were too feminine for me
I let them fall
I am strong

Life Letter

JAXON STEELE, age 16

Inspired by Tanner Z

If you're reading this,
I am still alive.
Still breathing through constricted lungs,
Even though sometimes I think I would rather be still.

I'm still hurting and suffering and fighting the encroaching
darkness.
I'm still having panic attacks and depressive episodes and
nightmares that wake me up in a cold sweat.
I'm still sparring with my inner demons and I'm still
dysphoric as all hell.
I'm still struggling to get out of bed in the morning.

I'm still afraid.

I'm still battling against my own mind.
The only difference is,
Now I'm finally gaining some ground.

I am still alive.

I'm still learning and exploring and laughing.
I'm still creating and caring and loving with all my heart.
I'm still doing what I can to help others.
I'm still healing.

I am still writing my story.

I am still alive.

I'm now on my seventeenth orbit around the sun and I'm still here.
I never thought I would make it through my fourteenth.

I'm still here and I'm telling you my story.
Because maybe I'm still alive for a reason.
Maybe my purpose is to help others realize that suicide is not an option.
Maybe I'm here to tell them to write a life letter instead.

I'm now reading this,
Which means I'm still alive.
My heart is still beating even though my mind has been telling it to stop for the past eight years.
My lungs are still breathing even though I've imprisoned them within a tight binder.

My eyes are still opening and closing and taking in
new sights even though I have prayed countless times
to see only darkness.

Whether because of a miracle,
or sheer stubbornness,
I am still alive.

Although I still go through points of self-loathing, I am a work of art and I am allowed to love myself.

—*Alexander McIntyre*

I AM ART

ALEXANDER MCINTYRE, age 16

After New Year 2018, I tattooed the words *I AM ART* on my right ankle. The words are for me. They are not for attention or recognition, they are a reminder.

Through the period of coming out and living as transgender, I have had to relearn who I am as a person...because in being trans, it's almost guaranteed that you will have to. I did and still continue to.

With this being said, the words *I AM ART* are a reminder of validation. Validation of my gender, sexuality and identity. A reminder that I am worthy of love, help and self-care. A reminder that I, as a trans youth and valuable member of society, deserve to be listened to.

Although I still go through points of self-loathing, I am a work of art and I am allowed to love myself.

Isolation

ASA O'CONNOR-JAECKEL, age 13

Isolation is meant to represent shifting dynamics in social relationships during and after transition.

What Can I Do Now?

ASTRI JACK, child and youth mental health worker,
+ J. MATSUI DE ROO, registered clinical counselor and supervisor

1. **Find strength in your story.** Everyone has their own story for getting through hard times. Consider your own story. What are the strengths that helped you get through? Notice things you did or didn't do that helped you. Maybe you found other trans people online or in person to talk to, or made art or listened to music or held a pet. Whatever helped you get through is something that you can keep using.

2. **Share your truth.** You may have had adults or other people doubt who you are, which can increase dysphoria, anxiety and depression. Knowing who you are means celebrating your own identity, with whatever language or form of expression feels right for you. You can do this just for yourself, share it privately with someone trusted or express yourself more broadly if it feels safe and okay. You could include a private journal entry, in which you describe your gender and share your name and pronouns with someone trusted, or dress in a way that best reflects who you are.

3. **Build your support network.** Being connected with other people is an important way to take care of your mental health. Whether you have in-person friends, online connections or trusted adults, including counselors, teachers or family, it's important that you know who you can reach out to if you're struggling. Consider keeping a list of the people you trust handy, on your phone or a piece of paper, so you can look at it and reach out if you're having a tough time.

4. **Be gentle to yourself when anxious.** Anxiety is a normal response to difficult things, but sometimes our anxiety takes more space than is helpful. A small amount of anxiety can help us be alert and prepared, but sometimes anxiety gets too big and becomes distressing. One way you can reduce anxiety to manageable levels is to help your body feel calmer and safer by slowing it down a little. You can start simply. Find a space where you can be alone and take ten deep breaths. If you can do that, you've already helped bring the anxiety down a tiny bit. You may find it useful to practice breathing exercises, mindfulness exercises or anything else that helps you slow down and relax a little.

5. **Be kind to yourself when depressed.** When you're depressed, it can be hard to do anything, even get out of bed. And depression can make your brain believe that everything is awful and will never improve. Sending kind thoughts to yourself is something you can do even if depression has taken away all your energy. If it's hard to extend kindness to yourself while you're depressed, try this mental trick: Imagine that your depressed self is a small animal. Are you a moping pup, a tired kitten, a worried hedgehog, a self-protective turtle, a tiny hiding bug? Whatever creature you imagine, think kind thoughts about it. Let the creature know that it is valued and loved, that it's okay to not be okay right now and that this feeling won't last forever. If you can form a mental image of the creature while having these thoughts, watch and see if it changes when you direct these thoughts of kindness to it.

What Can I Read Next?

PICTURE BOOKS

Howley, Jonty. *Big Boys Cry*. New York, NY: Random House, 2019.

Thorn, Theresa. *It Feels Good to Be Yourself: A Book about Gender Identity*. New York, NY: Henry Holt & Co., 2019.

YA AND GRAPHIC NOVELS

Madrone, Kelly Huegel. *LGBTQ: The Survival Guide for Lesbian, Gay, Bisexual, Transgender, and Questioning Teens*, 3rd ed. Minneapolis, MN: Free Spirit Publishing, 2018.

Emezi, Akwaeke. *Pet*. New York, NY: Penguin Random House, 2020.

GENERAL AUDIENCE

Fitzpatrick, Cat, and Casey Plett, eds. *Meanwhile, Elsewhere: Science Fiction and Fantasy from Transgender Writers*. New York, NY: Topside Press, 2017.

Singh, Annaliese. *The Queer & Transgender Resilience Workbook: Skills for Navigating Sexual Orientation and Gender Expression*. Oakland, CA: New Harbinger Publications, 2018.

Wilson-Yang, Jia Qing. *Small Beauty*. Montreal, QC: Metonymy Press, 2018.

MEMOIRS/FIRST-PERSON NARRATIVES

Bennett, Andrea. *Like a Boy But Not a Boy: Navigating Life, Mental Health, and Parenthood Outside the Gender Binary.* Vancouver, BC: Arsenal Pulp Press, 2020.

Ferguson, Joshua Marki. *Me, Myself, They: A Non-Binary Life.* Toronto, ON: House of Anansi Press, 2019.

Shraya, Vivek. *I'm Afraid of Men.* Toronto, ON: Penguin Canada, 2018. **Also available in French*

Violet, Mia. *Yes, You Are Trans Enough: My Transition from Self-Loathing to Self-Love.* London, UK: Jessica Kingsley Publishers, 2018.

Self-Portrait

AJAM, age 14

Acceptance

Many of the youth in this chapter chose to write letters to or about themselves before they knew they were trans. If you could speak with your own younger self, what would you say? How might you be different from the person your younger self expected you to be?

The chapter title, "Acceptance," brings to mind acceptance from parents and peers. However, most of the youth in this chapter chose to respond to the idea of self-acceptance. Why do you think that might be?

What patterns, similarities and differences do you see in how the youth think about and practice acceptance? Do any of these resonate with your own life?

Dear Grace

DAVID LLEWELYN, age 14

Dear Grace,

How have you been?

I haven't heard from you recently, but I suppose that's all right.
I'm glad I got to watch you grow up, but I'm thankful that
you're letting me stand in the spotlight now.

It was inspiring to see you evolve and change.
I watched you grow more comfortable with yourself, find
people and activities that made you happy.
You discovered things about yourself that you'd never dreamed
of, and in doing that, you found me.
So thanks for doing that and bringing me to the light.

People miss you.
They miss seeing you in class or around town.
Sometimes people ask me what happened.
I simply tell them that your time was up.

I don't miss you at all.
Every time I hear your name, it hurts me.
But not a sad kind of hurt.

Not an "I miss you, please come back" kind of hurt.
It's a "Don't remind me of that person" kind of hurt.

Thank you for leaving so I could stay.
It really means a lot to me.

Sincerely,
David

PS. Even though it might have seemed like I did at times,
I never hated you.

> Every time I hear your name, it hurts me.
> But not a sad kind of hurt.
> Not an "I miss you, please come
> back" kind of hurt.
> It's a "Don't remind me of that
> person" kind of hurt.
> Thank you for leaving so I could stay.
> It really means a lot to me.
> —David Llewelyn

The word is *boy*. I get addicted to it the summer I cut my hair short. I say it to myself in the mirror a thousand times. I say it to my friends as a joke that never lands. Again and again, I say it. In the sun, it seems like the perfect word, lit beautifully in the golden hues of killing time. But when the fall comes, I wonder if I dreamt it.

—*Christopher*

The Personal Dictionary of a Trans Semanticist

CHRISTOPHER, age 17

The word is *activist*. It's clunky, foreign, too big for my mouth to say, yet it follows me like a heavy debt. You won't see me with the picketers, but still they tell me every breath I take is something radical; every heartbeat, inexorably political. And so, I, the activist, go to class in the mornings, take a seat in the back and keep my head down until I get home.

The word is *boy*. I get addicted to it the summer I cut my hair short. I say it to myself in the mirror a thousand times. I say it to my friends as a joke that never lands. Again and again, I say it. In the sun, it seems like the perfect word, lit beautifully in the golden hues of killing time. But when the fall comes, I wonder if I dreamt it.

The word is *cowboy*. I remember it now: something I abandoned in the playground with the rest of my childhood wonders, laid to rest in a sandbox or a castle made of plastic. Dusting off old picture frames, I find it as it was—a declaration of make-believe identity that was endearingly misinformed then, questionably prophetic now. I shake it like an eight ball and beg it to answer all my questions. No reply.

The word is *40 percent*. It is our infamous number, our dancing death toll, ever-changing but never resolved. It is 40 percent of us who nearly lose ourselves to the fray we've gotten caught in. It is 40 percent of us who stop to wonder if this planet would be better off without us. And even that number, hanging overhead like the world's most precarious chandelier, can't stop me from putting the pieces together.

The word is **hormone replacement therapy**, written in the neon letters of a new headliner on Broadway. It is bright, electric, fantastic, and it arrives like an armistice amid chaos. It cures me of nothing, but teaches me, slowly, to do all the things I thought I couldn't: I speak to crowds, I shake strangers' hands, I look myself in the eyes. I breathe.

The word is *man*. For the longest time I don't know what it means. It is something made of stone when I am made of sand; it is something that burrows underground when I finally reach the mountaintop. They can call me a fool for trying, but I'll chase it all my life if it means catching up to it, just once.

The word is *strange*. I get used to it like I get used to shots in the leg and those real or imagined double takes in the bathroom. At first it stings like all words of its kind, all shots, all glances, but time erodes it into something oddly comforting. It is only a side effect of my freedom, and it won't be the last word I learn to stop hiding from.

The word is *trans*. For fourteen years I don't understand it. For two years I flinch when I hear it. For one year I scream it like I'm running out of breath. Now it sits easy in the concavity of a smile, comfortable on my tongue. I realize it is not a loaded weapon but an answer, finally, to a question that is not impossible anymore.

Sarah: A Trans Girl's Story

ALEXANDER M-G, age 13

Author's note: This story is one I made up — it's not REAL

Sarah walked down the street like always, scared and depressed.

"Hey, loser," a guy walking down the street said to her.

She ignored him. Sarah was trans and gay. She hated people bullying her. Her parents didn't support LGBTQ+ people. They still don't.

Her name is Sarah. It used to be Samuel, Sam for short. She was born a boy, but she goes by Sarah at school. Her parents don't know. Since she was four, she's thought she was a girl. "Mama," she would say, "I'm a girl."

"No," her mom would say. "You're a little boy."

"That's right," her dad would say.

Ugh, she thought, thinking about that moment. She was running away from home because her parents didn't care about her. Ever since the day before, when she told them she was trans and gay.

Sarah is only fourteen. She's in grade eight, in middle school. Her parents only care about her older sister, Chloe, since she told them. Chloe is nineteen. She does not support Sarah either.

An old woman grabbed Sarah's arm. "Where are you running off to?"

"Why do you want to know?" said Sarah, trying to yank her arm back.

The woman wouldn't let go. "Answer me," she said.

"I'm running away from home," Sarah blurted out.

"Why?" said the woman.

"Because my family doesn't care about me anymore," Sarah said.

"Oh, why?" the woman said.

"Because I'm trans." It was hard for Sarah to tell that to a complete stranger.

"Oh," the women said, and she loosened her grip while she thought about what Sarah said.

Sarah ran far away. She ran to a hotel close to her friend's house. Her friend Zoey and her family support Sarah and the LGBTQ+ community. Sarah brought money, so she checked in and lay on her hotel bed. She fell asleep and dreamed of a world where everyone was supportive of the LGBTQ+ community. She woke up and realized it was morning. She went to her friend Zoey's house and asked if she could live there forever. They understood her story and let her stay.

Genderfluid

HOPE, age 15

How I saw myself
I hated how my hair
Was down and long
I thought it would be better
Short and up

Ponytail, bun, beanie
My hair tucked away
It looked better
I looked better

I felt more masculine
Not so feminine
I began to love it
More and more

Though questions had to be asked
"Why do you keep your hair up so much?"
"Why do you wear that beanie so much?"
"It looks nice down."

For years I wore that beanie
My hair hidden away
It was two years later
Someone told me what

I had been feeling
An actual term, definition
For what I had
Been feeling

In my own body
What it meant to me
In my heart

I knew the feeling was true
I am **genderfluid**
I feel masculine at times
Then feminine too

I get good days
I get bad days
And days I don't know
How I feel

But I make it through
In my hard times

She. Her.
They. Them.
He. Him.

I find it hard at times
What can feel right with
My gender

What makes me happy
Is how I feel at the end of the day

Knowing I went out
Out in the world
As myself and not someone else

I am genderfluid
And that is a wonderful
Thing.

My name is Tor

My pronouns are he/they

Trans youth are cool

LEARN
LIVE
HOPE

Trans Is Beautiful

Trans Guys Are Real Guys

Embroidery

TOR BROUGHTON, age 12

What Can I Do Now?

ALYX MACADAMS, program facilitator for trans children and their parents/
primary caregivers

*I am no longer accepting the things I cannot change. I am changing
the things I cannot accept* —Angela Y. Davis

Affirmation is an inward practice that reverberates outward.
Affirmations can be validations that we carry with us, a way of
setting daily intentions or a tool we can turn to in moments of
need. The affirmations that follow are about cultivating abun-
dant acceptance in yourself and in others. They can be copied
so that they are available as inspiration or as reminders to help
you stay grounded in the work of accepting and supporting
trans youth. Explore different ways of using these affirmations (and add more!), but here are some ideas to help get you
started. You can draw an affirmation when you wake up and
notice when it comes up for you throughout your day, or use
affirmations as conversation starters with friends, trans youth
and family members. You can make this a creative and crafty
project by writing out the affirmations and making them look
fancy and spectacular. Most important? Accept the journey
these affirmations take you on.

AFFIRMATIONS FOR ABUNDANT ACCEPTANCE

1. **I accept that I have a role to play in resisting discrimination against trans youth because all inequity and injustice is unacceptable.** I acknowledge that systems of violence are rooted in **settler colonialism** and disproportionately target Two-Spirit, trans and nonbinary Black, Indigenous and People of Color. I accept my responsibility to learn about and resist all structures of violence and oppression, even if I'm not directly affected.

2. **I accept trans youth as the experts of their own lives.** I accept that I don't need to be an expert to be a support to trans youth.

3. **I accept that I will have to unlearn some of my beliefs about gender.** I've learned some prejudices and stereotypes that are harmful to trans people. I accept that any lack of knowledge about gender diversity is not a personal shortcoming, but is an occasion for personal growth.

4. I accept that struggling for social change can be difficult and exhausting, and I will be gentle with myself in this work. I accept that witnessing trans youth experience erasure and violence, barriers to care and rejection from those who should love them will make my mind, heart and body ache. I will remember that this is a collective heartache that can bring me closer to those I am fighting for.

5. I accept that I will be transformed by the magic of having young trans people in my life. I celebrate this, and I celebrate them.

What Should I Read Next?

PICTURE BOOKS

Hirst, Jo. *A House for Everyone: A Story To Help Children Learn About Gender Identity and Gender Expression.* London, UK: Jessica Kingsley Publishers, 2018.

Love, Jessica. *Julián Is a Mermaid.* London, UK: Walker Books, 2018. **Also available in French*

Roher, Megan. *Is It a Boy, Girl or Both?* San Francisco, CA: Wilgefortis Press, 2016.

YA AND GRAPHIC NOVELS

Rose, Syan. *Our Work Is Everywhere: An Illustrated Oral History of Queer & Trans Resistance.* Vancouver, BC: Arsenal Pulp Press, 2021.

Stevenson, Robin. *Pride: The Celebration and the Struggle.* Victoria, BC: Orca Book Publishers, 2020.

GENERAL AUDIENCE

Tannehill, Brynn. *Everything You Ever Wanted to Know about Trans (But Were Afraid to Ask).* London, UK: Jessica Kingsley Publishers, 2019.

Thom, Kai Cheng. *I Hope We Choose Love: A Trans Girl's Notes from the End of the World.* Vancouver, BC: Arsenal Pulp Press, 2019.

MEMOIRS/FIRST-PERSON NARRATIVES

Dugan, Jess. T., and Vanessa Fabbre. *To Survive on This Shore: Photographs and Interviews with Transgender and Gender Nonconforming Older Adults*. Heidelberg, Germany: Kehrer Vertag, 2019.

Tobia, Jacob. *Sissy: A Coming-of-Gender Story*. New York, NY: G.P. Putnam's Sons, 2019.

I am genderfluid
I feel masculine at times
Then feminine too
I get good days
I get bad days
And days I don't know
How I feel
But I make it through
In my hard times
She. Her.
They. Them.
He. Him.

—*Hope*

Afterword

A Binary Binder

GLYNNE EVANS, age 74

My brother wears a frilly dress
An auntie goes by "he"
I can be gender neutral—
Until I have to pee.

Ditch the Straights' Jacket

GLYNNE EVANS, age 74

Mother was scared of the neighbors
Dad rolled his eyes far away
The principal said, "Just a phase, I suppose"
Most kids just thought I was gay

Well, the neighbors felt sorry for Mother
or wanted to know all the "dirt"
Dad was "sure we aren't Scottish"
So I "shouldn't be wearing a skirt"

One kid thinks I'm a really great rebel
and my bravery's really cool too
My teach says, "It's gone far enough now"—
she's afraid we'll meet in the loo

Though I've known I am trans for years now
my parents I never dared tell
When I did, they said I am selfish
and surely I'd go straight to hell

I told them I'd not go anywhere straight, thanks
and what hell they were making for me
stop treating me, please, like merely a chattel
and refer to me, kindly, as "she"

The shrink said, "Nothing will work here"
To make me "normal as most"
So my parents must learn to accept me
Or I must accept that I'm toast

A trans friend who is old and a rock of support
and cheerful in spite of it all
has told me to grow a very thick skin
But if needed, show flashes of gall

She's had her "phase" now for decades
and it certainly isn't a sham
so "passing" is not what the "phase" did
Passing will affirm who I am

Now, trans are musicians and singers
politicians and athletes, and it's true!
Even bosses are beginning to hire us!
Will that give my parents a clue?

Editors' note: There is no one "right" way to write an author bio. Just like the trans youth themselves and the stories they shared in this book, there's lots of diversity. Some authors wrote a lot about themself, others wrote very little. A few chose not to write a bio at all.

Meet the Contributors

A.J. Gabriel is a 17-year-old writer who goes by *he/him/his* pronouns and strongly dislikes writing in the third person. Unfortunately, he also enjoys fueling his inner rage, so he will continue to write this as though he were someone else. A.J. identifies as male and lives his life as a regular dude, despite his doctor sending him on a different path at birth. He could go on and on about how he decided to turn his assigned identity on its head, but that is not why we are here at the moment. You picked up this book, and we are so very grateful that you are taking time to take a look at the works of a bunch of queer teens. Of course, A.J. is not a professional anything—he could be considered a professional procrastinator, though—and is not here to tell you what you can and can't do. He simply wishes to express his passion for how important self-love and self-care are. Loving yourself and caring for yourself are so important, and A.J. hopes to reach out to those who come across his work and encourages people to remain curious.

Ajam (any pronouns) is a ***genderqueer*** artist living in Victoria, BC. From a very young age the story of Peter Pan has been a major influence on their art and their gender experience. As part of the Gender Generations Project, they are working with politicians to help create better policies for BC's trans youth. Peace out!

Alexander M-G is a trans male, he is 13, he lives in Victoria, BC, and he likes reading, writing, fencing, swimming and horseback riding. His favorite books are the Darkness Rising trilogy.

Alexander McIntyre is a 16-year-old transgender boy living in Slocan Valley, BC. He is an experienced creative writer and multimedia artist who is also very involved in the theater community. He is fairly new to the transgender community, but has worked hard to spread awareness about LGBTQ+ acceptance in his rural location.

Alyx MacAdams is a settler of Gaelic Scottish, Irish and English ancestry, living in the traditional territory of the Lekwungen peoples. Their Master of Social Work thesis centered on a critical analysis of how trans children's experiences of care are shaped by and resist normative citizenship, settler colonialism and neoliberalism. A typical and of course reluctant-to-admit-it Aquarian (sun and ascendant), Alyx has always been interested in issues of justice and social change. This has taken them on a wandering road of organizing and working as a facilitator, youth worker, outdoor educator and anti-violence worker. These days they can be found facilitating programs for trans children and their parents/primary caregivers, doting on their plants and filling their heart with the joyous wonders of co-parenting a young child.

Asa O'Connor-Jaeckel is a 13-year-old, carbon-based life form living with their parents and pot plants in Victoria, BC. They enjoy reading, writing, acting, drawing, running around open fields like an insane chicken, jumping off high things, contemplating the existence of everything and, of course, consuming pickles. They are often found singing as loud as they can and rummaging through recycling bins for makeshift bookmarks.

Astri Jack (*she/her*) is a queer, cisgender woman and white settler living on the traditional lands of the Kosampson family of the Lekwungen peoples (Victoria, BC). Astri works in child and youth mental health and is passionate about play, arts and narrative-based therapies. She is also a qualitative researcher in the fields of mental health, queer identity, and children, youth and families. She is committed to anti-oppressive, intersectional approaches in her practice and believes that social justice work that upholds the inherent dignity of all beings is our most powerful tool for creating lasting and meaningful change.

Christopher is a 17-year-old high school student from Nanaimo, BC. He is passionate about creative writing and working with youth, and in his spare time he is (very, very slowly) teaching himself to play the guitar. He hopes his writing will help reassure young trans kids while also humanizing the trans experience for those who struggle to understand it.

Christopher Wolff (*he/him/they/them* pronouns) is a trans writer, facilitator and educator living and working on Coast Salish territory as an immigrant from western Europe. Besides having had the pleasure of being an adult mentor for the Trans Tipping Point, now called the Gender Generations Project, Christopher has also been involved with several community organizations in Vancouver, BC, where they have worked to improve access and services for queer and trans folks. Christopher is currently doing research on the cultural and social history of transgender artists. In his spare time, they attempt to finish the various novels he has started writing.

Danny Charles is a young, Indigenous, female-to-male guy who uses *he/him* pronouns. He is from Victoria, BC, is 17 years old and loves painting, working with kids, dad jokes and puns.

David Llewelyn is a 14-year-old trans guy who uses *he/him* pronouns. He was born and raised in Victoria, BC, and writes anything from short stories to emotionally charged persuasive essays about the failings of DC movies. In his spare time David enjoys playing guitar, working with chain mail and making sarcastic comments at the back of his classes. He also enjoys memorizing useless information, such as the registry number on the Starship *Enterprise* (which, in case you were wondering, is NCC-1701).

Dylan Ariawan is an 18-year-old artist from Nanaimo, BC. He is currently studying clinical psychology and visual arts at university. His artworks are a combination of abstract realism, minimalism, conceptual and also personal. He aspires to one day be able to help people in their emotional challenges through works of art.

Finn Lewis is 13 years old. He lives in the Greater Vancouver area of British Columbia. He is passionate about art and spends his time creating comic-style, hand-drawn characters. Nearly all of Finn's characters and storylines center around LGBTQ themes. His hope is that one day these stories might help "normalize" LGBTQ people and eliminate the stigma surrounding them.

Glynne Evans uses female pronouns but will respond to any if food is offered. She is a 74-year-old white settler somewhat embarrassed by her white privilege and by her delaying from the age of 3 until age 66 to act on her gender self-knowledge. She is heartened by the remarkably kind reception she has had from her pre- and post-transition friends and acquaintances, especially in the context of being a privileged white settler among poorly treated Indigenous folks and other disadvantaged groups. Her main preoccupations are doing her tiny bit to mitigate climate change and helping reduce exposure to the pandemic among the most endangered. Glynne's verses in the Afterword are not in the least bit autobiographical, except in the direction of the gender change.

Hope is 15 years old and goes by the pronouns *they/them/theirs*. They are from Victoria, BC. Hope got into writing when they were 14 and started doing poems when they were 15. Hope has always enjoyed writing as a break from stress and anxiety. Writing has helped them through a lot.

J. Matsui De Roo is a registered clinical counselor, clinical supervisor and consultant in private practice. A mixed-race Japanese Canadian, queer, nonbinary settler, Matsui lives and works on the ancestral, unceded lands of the Musqueam, Squamish and Tsleil-Waututh First Nations. Matsui's work is grounded in anti-oppression theory and practice. Areas of focus include resilience and healing from trauma, abuse and oppression; honoring intersectional queer, trans and gender-diverse identities; resisting ableism when living with chronic pain, disability and illness; and celebrating sexual health, wellness and pleasure.

Dr. Jake Pyne is an assistant professor in the York University School of Social Work. As an advocate in Toronto's trans community for 20 years, Jake has worked on projects to improve access to healthcare, housing and emergency shelter, family law justice and support for gender-independent children and trans youth. His doctoral research explored thinkable futures for trans youth and brought together transgender studies, critical disability studies, critical autism studies, fat studies and queer of color critique. Jake's current research (on dis/human others) explores the intersection of autistic and trans life.

Jasper Ledgerwood is a 14-year-old trans writer living in Windsor, Ontario, and trying their best in life. They go by *he/him* and *they/them* pronouns, and they really love cats. They hope this book will raise awareness about the trans community.

Jaxon Steele is a 16-year-old raised in the Okanagan Valley of BC. He enjoys long hikes with his dog, exploring new places and spending time with his group of ultra queer friends. Through his writing, he hopes to reassure and affirm other trans youth while they are navigating the treacherous waters of growing up in a binary, cis-centric world.

Kyle Shaughnessy is a Two-Spirit, trans person of mixed Indigenous (Dene) and European ancestry. He is a social worker and writer originally from the Northwest Territories and small-town BC and has been supporting trans and Two-Spirit youth and their families since the early 2000s. He works in the public healthcare system as an educator on trans and Two-Spirit wellness. Kyle has an ever-increasing appreciation for the experiences he has witnessed and history he holds as a now middle-aged member of Vancouver's trans community and feels deep honor in working alongside youth on intergenerational community projects.

Dr. Lee Airton is an assistant professor of Gender and Sexuality Studies in Education at Queen's University, which is situated on traditional Anishinaabe and Haudenosaunee territory in Katarokwi-Kingston, Ontario. As a teacher educator and nonbinary person who uses *they/them* pronouns, Lee is proud and delighted to know the youth who are part of the TTP (GGP) and hopes to see some of them in teachers college someday. From 2012 to 2019, Lee ran They Is My Pronoun, a Q+A-based blog about gender-neutral pronoun usage and user support with over 30,000 unique visitors in 2017 alone. Lee is also the founder of the No Big Deal Campaign, a national social media initiative that helps people show support for transgender people's right to have their pronouns used. In recognition of their advocacy work, Lee received a 2017 Youth Role Model of the Year Award from the Canadian Centre for Gender and Sexual Diversity. Lee's first book, *Gender: Your Guide; A Gender-Friendly Primer on What to Know, What to Say and What to Do in the New Gender Culture,* offers practical steps for welcoming gender diversity in all areas of everyday life and is available from Adams Media. With Dr. Susan Woolley, they are also the editor of *Teaching about Gender Diversity: Teacher-Tested Lesson Plans for K-12 Classrooms* (Canadian Scholars Press).

Lindsay Cavanaugh is a full-time PhD student at the Ontario Institute for Studies in Education (OISE) at the University of Toronto. She studies queer and decolonial ways of teaching and learning. Lindsay is a white settler, cisgender and queer educator of Irish, French and British ancestry. She has taught high school learners on Lekwungen territory in Victoria, BC, and Anishinaabe territory in a remote Oji-Cree community in Ontario called North Spirit Lake First Nation. She is passionate about supporting trans, nonbinary, Two-Spirit and queer educators and youth navigating K-12 schools and about changing education systems so they are more affirming places. Lindsay volunteers with the Queering Schools Network, which is a local collective of LGBTQIA2S+ educators and youth in Victoria, BC, that emerged from her participatory master's project.

Luna Orion is from the depths of the Fraser Valley and is a flourishing nonbinary writer who is 14 years old and goes by *they/them* pronouns. They love all things queer, nerdy and musical. They hope their contributions to the Gender Generations Project help create more understanding of nonbinary identities.

Lupus is a 14-year-old, trans, nonbinary individual who goes by *they/them* pronouns. Born and raised in Alberta, they write stories in many different genres and styles—comics, short stories, fantasy and fiction. As a young author, they have no lack of creative inspiration and write every week. Lupus hopes this anthology of writing helps change the perspectives of other young, queer individuals and helps them discover more about themselves.

Maisie Bodrug (*she/her/hers*) is 13 and lives in Victoria, BC. She won the Victoria Pride Society's OutWrite eZine competition and read her winning poems at the Pride in the Word event in 2018. She has also presented her poetry at the OUTstages. Her visual art has been displayed at the University of Victoria Legacy Art Gallery from the second Gender Generations Project event. She wants to study anthropology in university one day and travel to Japan.

Max is a 13-year-old transgender student, writer and artist from Squamish, BC. He has very strong views about the fact that Pluto is a planet, even if some people say it isn't [*Editors' note: It isn't* ☺]. Max advocates for transgender rights and hopes to be able to do more in the future.

Owen Miller is a 16-year-old STEM student in Victoria, BC. As an openly transgender male, he works toward gender-variance awareness within schools and through BC legislation. He loves his family and is especially enthusiastic about chemistry. He hopes to develop and improve treatment for people in transition.

Samuel Busch is a 17-year-old artist of all kinds who lives in the very western part of Canada. He/they love(s) to write poetry, stream-of-consciousness works and multimedia art journals.

Tash McAdam is a Welsh-Canadian educator, activist and author. They write fast-paced, plot-focused young adult fiction centering marginalised identities. More about their writing can be found at tashmcadam.com. They were the first mentor on board with the Trans Tipping Point, now called the Gender Generations Project, and it has been a life-changing and -affirming experience for them. They're usually found lost in a book or their own head.

Tor Broughton is an advocate for transgender youth in the Okanagan region of BC. He is a TedX presenter, public speaker and trans-rights activist. He loves football, music, writing and flipping. Tor is 12 years old and has been out and proud for three of those years. He loves his supportive friends and family, and has always had a passion for storytelling.

Yakusinn DeBoer is a nonbinary person from Kelowna, BC, who loves to view and experience others' art. They are 18 years old and like spending their time honing their artistic skills in every medium, including digital painting, music and writing.

Resources We Love

Resources and Services for Trans Youth and the Adults Who Love Them

gegi.ca: A comprehensive tool kit to help you or a loved one advocate for your gender-expression and gender-identity human rights at school, with info specific to each Ontario school board. Relevant to other provinces and territories as well. gegi.ca

Gender Creative Kids: Evidence-based resources for gender-creative kids and their families, schools and communities. All materials also available in French. gendercreativekids.ca

Gender Spectrum: Information to create gender-sensitive and inclusive environments for all children and teens. genderspectrum.org

InterACT: Advocacy, resources and services for *intersex* youth and those who love them. interactadvocates.org

It Gets Better Project: Aims to uplift, empower and connect lesbian, gay, bisexual, transgender and queer (LGBTQ+) youth around the globe. itgetsbetter.org

MOSAIC Trans Newcomers Resource Hub: Online community, resources and peer support for trans newcomers to Canada. mosaicbc.org/resources/trans

Native Youth Sexual Health Network: Online resources and services for Two-Spirit youth and their families and caregivers. nativeyouthsexualhealth.com

PFLAG Canada: National organization that offers peer-to-peer support to help people with issues of sexual orientation, gender identity and gender expression. Chapters all across Turtle Island in Canada and the United States. pflag.ca

Q Chat Space: Digital LGBTQ+ center where teens join live-chat, professionally facilitated online support groups. qchatspace.org

QMUNITY: British Columbia's queer, trans and Two-Spirit resource center, located in Coast Salish territory in Vancouver, BC. qmunity.ca

Rainbow Health Ontario: Information about LGBTQ health and links to LGBTQ-friendly physical and mental health services in Ontario. rainbowhealthontario.ca

Sex & U: Run by the Society of Obstetricians and Gynaecologists of Canada, this site provides accurate, credible and up-to-date information and education on topics related to sexual and reproductive health. sexandu.ca

SOGI 123: Helps educators and parents make schools inclusive and safe for students of all sexual orientations and gender identities (SOGI). sogieducation.org

Trans Care BC: BC-wide hub providing information about gender-affirming care and support. phsa.ca/our-services/programs-services/trans-care-bc

Trans Life Line: Crisis line for trans and questioning people, staffed 24 hours a day by trans-identified volunteers. 1-877-330-6366. translifeline.org

Transforming Hearts Collective: Intersectional supports and resources for faith communities looking to become more LGB and trans welcoming, inclusive and affirming. transformingheartscollective.org

Urban Native Youth Association 2-Spirit Collective: Provides support, resources and programming for Indigenous youth ages 15 to 30 who identify as Two-Spirit or LGBTQ+ (lesbian, gay, bisexual, transgender, queer, gender nonconforming, along with many other identities) and to those who are questioning their sexual or gender identities. unya.bc.ca/programs/2-spirit-collective

Research Institutes about Trans Youth

Family Acceptance Project: Strength-based research about trans youth and their families, schools, religious groups and other institutions. familyproject.sfsu.edu

Stigma and Resilience Among Vulnerable Youth Centre: Rigorous, award-winning research on how stigma, discrimination, violence and trauma affect young Canadians' health, including factors that foster youth resilience in spite of stigma. saravyc.ubc.ca

Trans PULSE: A community-based research project investigating the impact of social exclusion and discrimination on the health of trans people in Ontario. Findings are relevant for other provinces and territories. transpulseproject.ca

Trans Youth CAN!: Multidisciplinary team of academic, clinical, service-provider and knowledge-user partners studying healthcare for trans youth and effects on their families across Canada. transyouthcan.ca

Pronoun-Specific Resources

My Pronouns: Everything you ever wanted to know about pronouns. mypronouns.org

No Big Deal Campaign: Free posters and printables to get comfortable with pronouns. nbdcampaign.ca

They Is My Pronoun: Interactive guide to incorporate all-gender pronouns in everyday life. theyismypronoun.com

Terms To Know

TASH MCADAM

ally—someone who is not part of a marginalized group but supports that group's civil rights and actively works toward equality. For example, Rick Riordan is an ally to queer and trans folk. He includes authentic, three-dimensional queer and trans characters in his books.

binder—a tight-fitting item of clothing worn on the upper body to give the appearance of a flat/flatter chest

biological sex—a medical term used to classify a person as female or male or **intersex.** Alternate terms include sex, physical sex, anatomical sex or sex assigned/designated at birth (AFAB stands for assigned female at birth, AMAB for assigned male at birth).

BIPOC—acronym for Black, Indigenous and People of Color. POC (people of color) is often used as an umbrella term to describe nonwhite people.

The acronym attempts to highlight the particular racism and injustices that impact all people of color, especially Black and Indigenous people.

blocker—hormone blocker (also known as a puberty blocker), a drug that delays puberty. Hormone blockers are prescribed to pubescent youth who may or may not choose to pursue **hormone replacement therapy (HRT)** later in life. The effects of hormone blockers are temporary and reversible.

cisgender—relating to or being a person whose *gender identity* corresponds with their *biological sex*. *Cis* (sounds like *sis*) means "on this side of" in Latin. When we use cis to talk about a person, we mean that they are not trans.

gender binary—the concept that there are only two distinct genders, male and female (*binary* means "two things"). The gender binary excludes **trans** people.

gender dysphoria—the state of feeling that one's **gender identity** does not match one's **biological sex**. This can cause depression, anxiety and lots of other issues for **trans** people.

gender expression—how an individual presents their gender outwardly through appearance, dress, behavior, etc. Someone who expresses their gender in a more feminine way is said to be "feminine presenting," while someone who expresses their gender in a more masculine way is "masculine presenting."

gender identity—a person's sense of themself as boy/man, girl/woman, both or neither.

genderfluid—a term that describes a gender identity that shifts between masculine and feminine from day to day.

genderqueer—a person who does not identify with the **gender binary** of man/woman or an umbrella term

for many gender nonconforming or **nonbinary** identities.

homophobic—fear or hatred of people who are homosexual (sexually or romantically attracted to someone of the same sex). From the Greek words homos ("same") and phobos ("fear").

hormone replacement therapy (HRT)—treatment with hormones to align secondary sexual characteristics (such as fat distribution or hair growth) more closely with someone's **gender identity.**

intersectional—referencing the connection and overlap between different social categories, such as gender, race and class. *Intersectionality* illustrates the fact that these categories combine to create different systems of discrimination. For example, a Black trans woman may face significantly more discrimination than a Black man, a trans woman or a cis woman.

intersex—someone whose hormones, chromosomes or anatomy differ from the two expected patterns of male or female.

Lupron—a puberty-blocking hormone that prevents the physical changes associated with puberty. Using hormone **blockers** is often the first step in an ongoing medical transition.

misgender—to use words (often **pronouns** but also gendered forms of address, such as *Sir*) that incorrectly gender a person.

misogynist—a person who fears or hates women (based on the word *misogyny*, which comes from the Greek *miso*, meaning "hatred," and *gunē*, meaning "woman.") More commonly, in modern society, a misogynist is someone who has a dislike or contempt for women and/or femininity.

neurodiverse—characterized by neurologically atypical (not typical) patterns of thought or behavior. *Neuro* refers to the mind and *diverse* refers to diversity. A neurodiverse person is not *neurotypical*.

nonbinary—umbrella term for all genders other than female/male. Not every nonbinary person identifies as trans, and not all trans people identify as nonbinary.

patriarch—the male head of a family. *Patriarchy* refers to the system of society and government in which men largely hold the power and women and nonbinary and/or trans folks are excluded from positions of power.

privilege—the special rights or advantages of being part of a group that holds more power in society, such as white privilege, whereby white people are overrepresented in positions of power.

pronouns—words that take the place of nouns or noun phrases in a sentence. In the sentence "Marie is reading a book," the name Marie might be replaced by the pronoun *she*. Common singular pronouns (words to describe one person) include *he, she* and *they*, but there are many more pronouns used by trans people to define their gender, including *zi, zir* and *hir*.

queer—an umbrella term sometimes used to describe those people with nonconforming gender identities.

Because of its history of being used as a slur or hate speech, *queer* is still disliked in some parts of the LGBTQ2S+ community. The word should only be used for self-identification ("I am queer") or with consent ("My cousin is **genderqueer.**")

settler colonialism—the ongoing system of power that perpetuates the exploitation, genocide and repression of Indigenous Peoples and cultures. It is a form of colonialism that attempts to replace the Indigenous population with a settler population.

T—short for *testosterone*, the major male sex hormone. People who are incorrectly assigned female at birth (AFAB) may choose to take testosterone in order to masculinize their bodies.

transgender/trans—people whose gender identity doesn't match the sex they were assigned at birth. The opposite of **cis**. *Trans* or *transgender* has mostly replaced the word *transsexual*.

transition—moving or changing from one state to another. In terms of gender identity, transition usually denotes social changes (name, expression, appearance) and/or medical intervention, such as **HRT** or gender-affirming surgery.

transphobia—fear, hatred or dislike of transgender people, and/or prejudice and discrimination against them by individuals or institutions.

Two-Spirit—a modern umbrella term used by some Indigenous people in North America to describe people who have both a masculine and a feminine spirit. Also spelled as Two Spirit, two spirit or, occasionally, twospirited.

Acknowledgments

Growing Up Trans was at one point named after a project titled the Trans Tipping Point (TTP), now called the Gender Generations Project (GGP). It is an intergenerational community that serves trans youth. Mentors are the heart of the GGP, and without their generosity in relationship building and workshop programming, the GGP simply would not exist. We are grateful to the following mentors for their love and expertise over the years: Akira Imai, Al Cusack, Alexa McDaniel, Arran Liddel, Astrid Carter, Charlie/Henrietta Dubét, Chase Willier, Christopher Wolff, Cole Devoy, Dani Cooper, Gavin Somers, Jo Cuffe, Jo Nazatul, Julian Paquette, Kai Taddei, Kat Palmateer, Kori Doty, Laurie Feehan, Rose Cotton, Sabrina Symington, Serena Bhandar, Sophia Rawl, Tash McAdam, Will Weigler and Ziggy Schutz. In addition to the mentors, Morgane Oger and Dr. Lee Airton served as unifying, energizing and inspiring keynote speakers who gave us all new ways to think about trans activism, resistance and resilience.

If the mentors are the GGP's heart, then its volunteers are surely its backbone. Many of the following individuals, couples and families opened their homes and billeted youth and mentors and then rolled up their sleeves to run the kitchen. Behind the scenes they gave rides and swept floors, took out the garbage and set up tables. We are so grateful to Arran Liddel and Gen Walsh, Ashling Ligate and Beckham Ronaghan, Astri Jack and Ainsley Kling, Chava Nagalia, Darcy Allder and Heather Zeh-Allder, David Tillson, Glynne and Suzie Evans, Jordan Watters,

Katrina McGee and David, Sol, and Rosa Bodrug, Kelly Legge/ Persi Flage, Lindsay Cavanaugh, Macaulay Mauro, Morgan Brooks, Nickie and Tyler Lewis, Robin Stevenson and Cheryl May, Roe and Corrie Campbell, Sean Brown, Shahriar Khan, Whitney Walsh, Zinnia Clark and Tyler Schaus.

The GGP gratefully acknowledges and appreciates the monetary and in-kind donations of the following organizations who took a chance on a fledgling research project and whose material contributions made the magic happen: the British Columbia Teachers' Federation; the British Columbia Ministry of Children and Family Development; Community Cabbage; the Centre for Outreach Education at UVic; Vanya McDonell, Thomas King and the team at the Fairfield Gonzales Community Association; UVic's Legacy and Legacy Maltwood art galleries; Oregano's Pizza; PFLAG Victoria; Power to Be; the Tegan and Sara Foundation; Tessa McLoughlin and the team at KWENCH; Trans Care BC; Vancouver City Savings Credit Union; the Vancouver Island Public Interest Research Group; the Victoria Foundation and the Victoria Pride Society.

Finally, we are so appreciative of Kirstie, Dahlia, Andrew and the team at Orca Book Publishers for believing in this project and generously guiding it through to publication.

Kate:

I would like to first thank my former roommates at Bisley House: Haneen Ghebari, Dana Johnson, Bonnie Wearmouth and Amy Bader. They were not only hugely supportive during GGP's first year but also patiently put up with my antics and generously opened their home to house-visiting mentors. I'm appreciative of the support of my parents, Jake Fry and Dr. Beth Seaton. I feel lucky to have grown up in a household that was accepting of LGBTQ+ people well before I was born. My participation in this project was informed by the fantastic friends I've made throughout my life: Jae Levy, Kara Stanton, Kelly McLeod, Katie Hughes, Avery Burrow, Ciara Gordon, Evan Wendel and Gina Hay. I am constantly learning what community means from you. Last but certainly not least, huge thanks to Dr. Lindsay Herriot, who has been an incredible mentor to me and without whom I would never have had the opportunity to work on this extraordinary project.

Lindsay:

First and foremost, I'm appreciative of Lauren M., who shared the challenges and magic of gender transition with me so many years ago. Wishing that this book had existed when you were a little girl, or even when you were socially and medically transitioning as an adult, was in many ways the inspiration for this project. I am also grateful to long-time mentor Dr. Alan Sears, whose peerless example of how to build mentoring relationships informed the structure, process, research design and community-building of the GGP.

Working with co-founder and co-conspirator Kate Fry for all these years has been a dream come true. Not many people would turn a casual coffee conversation into a multi-year, fly-by-the-seat-of-your-pants adventure, but that's Kate. Thank you, Kate, for your friendship, spontaneity, inventiveness and quick wit. Likewise, considerable gratitude is owed to jack-of-all-trades Tash McAdam, who served as a founding mentor, volunteer, managing editor and problem solver extra-ordinaire. Your meticulous organizational skills and logistics wizardry are legendary. Thank you also to my colleagues Dr. Lee Airton, Don Cochrane and Dr. Kathy Sanford for believing in this new approach to participatory action research from its inception.

Every editor should be blessed with dear ones such as Amy Ashmore and Dr. James Grayson, Alison Zacharias, Caitlin Mooney, Dr. Paula Dubois and Dr. Rod Knight, who provided levity and cheerleading throughout. Furthermore, my folks, Blaine Lewis and Leone Wilkinson, took their usual enthusiastic encouragement of me to new levels by running errands, coordinating the pizza parties and barbecues, and being on grandparent duty so I could do this work. I was also lucky to be surrounded by a smattering of supportive siblings, such as my sister, Dr. Lara Hiseler, godsisters Bekah Sears and Dr. Dusty Johnstone, brothers Sean Lewis, Seth Bryant and Andrew Manderson, brother-in-law Rob Hiseler, and sisters-in-law Ana Manderson and Jody Reimer, who offered wisdom and mirth throughout.

On the home front, I am continually appreciative of my children, Finnegan and Corbin, who were so patient while I did this work. May the world you grow up in be filled with lots of joyful gender identities and expressions. Finally, I cherish the incalculable emotional and practical contributions of my long-suffering and good-humored spouse, Ryan. I am grateful to you most of all.

 Dr. Lindsay Herriot is a full-time inclusion/special education teacher in the Greater Victoria School District. She also works at the University of Victoria in several capacities, as an adjunct/sessional professor in both the Faculty of Education and the School of Child and Youth Care and as a fellow at the Centre for Studies in Religion and Society. A cisgender, bisexual, white settler, Lindsay is originally from unceded Mi'kmaq territory near Moncton, New Brunswick, and is of Acadian, Scottish and Anglo heritage. She now lives on the unceded territory of the Lekwungen Peoples in Victoria, British Columbia, with her spouse and two young children.

 Kate Fry is a writer and editor currently living as a white settler on the unceded lands of the Lekwungen Peoples. Her writing has appeared in several publications, including *Prism International, This Side of West, Bad Dog Review* and *The Albatross*. She recently completed a BA with honors in English literature from the University of Victoria. Kate co-founded the Trans Tipping Point, now called the Gender Generations Project, in 2017 with her great friend and mentor, Lindsay Herriot.

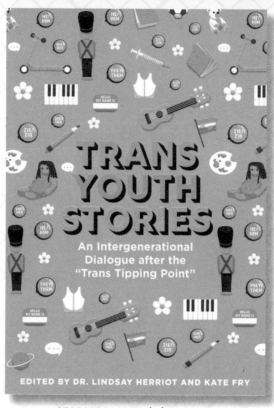